HEBREW
MANUSCRIPT PAINTING

HEBREW MANUSCRIPT PAINTING

Joseph Gutmann

GEORGE BRAZILLER NEW YORK

To Marilyn

Published in 1978.

For information address the publisher:
George Braziller, Inc.
One Park Avenue, New York, New York 10016

Library of Congress Cataloging in Publication Data

Gutmann, Joseph, 1923–
Hebrew manuscript painting.

Bibliography: p. 33
1. Illumination of books and manuscripts, Jewish.
2. Illumination of books and manuscripts, Medieval.
I. Title.
ND2935.G79 745.6'7 78–3643
ISBN 0–8076–0890–4
ISBN 0–8076–0891–2 pbk.

First Edition

Printed by Imprimeries Réunies in Switzerland

DESIGNED BY RANDALL DE LEEUW

CONTENTS

ACKNOWLEDGMENTS

I am deeply indebted to Professors Stanley F. Chyet, Robert Nelson, and Mirella Levi D'Ancona for their gracious assistance, and to the staff at George Braziller, especially Adele Westbrook and Andrea Kaliski, for their careful attention to the many aspects of this book.

The author and publishers would also like to express their sincere thanks to the following institutions and individuals who kindly provided materials and granted permission to reproduce them in this volume.

Color Plates

BOLOGNA, Biblioteca Universitaria di Bologna, Plate 35 (Photo, Cav. Uff. Umberto Orlandini, Modena).

BUDAPEST, Library of the Hungarian Academy of Sciences, Plate 23 (Photo, Interfoto MTI, Budapest).

COPENHAGEN, The Royal Library, Plate 22.

DARMSTADT, Hessische Landes-und Hochschulbibliothek, Plate 29 (Photo, Charles V. Passela, New York).

HAMBURG, Staats-und Universitätsbibliothek, Plates 30, 31.

JERUSALEM, Israel Museum, Plates 37, 38.

JERUSALEM, Jewish National and University Library, Plate 5 (Photo, David Harris, Jerusalem).

JERUSALEM, Schocken Institute, Plate 18 (Photo, David Harris, Jerusalem).

LEIPZIG, Karl-Marx-Universitätsbibliothek, Plates 24, 25, 26 (Photo, Edition Leipzig).

LISBON, Biblioteca Nacional de Lisboa, Plate 10 (Photo, Laboratórios Fototécnicos, Limitada).

LONDON, Reproduced by permission of the British Library Board, Plates 1, 2, 11, 12, 19, 20, 21, 27, 28, 32.

MANCHESTER, The John Rylands University Library, Plates 13, 14.

MUNICH, Bayerische Staatsbibliothek, Plate 17.

PARIS, Bibliothèque Nationale, Plates 6, 7, 39, 40.
PARMA, Biblioteca Palatina, Plates 8, 9 (Photo, Vaghi Fotoprodotti, Parma).
ROME, Biblioteca Apostolica Vaticana, Plates 33, 34.
ROVIGO, Biblioteca dell Accademia dei Concordi, Plate 36 (Photo, Mario Piombo & Siviero, Rovigo).
SARAJEVO, Zemaljski Musej, Plates 15, 16 (Photo, Charles V. Passela, New York).
TÜBINGEN, Universitätsbibliothek, Plates 3, 4 (Photo, Staatsbibliothek Preussischer Kulturbesitz, Berlin).

Black-and-White Figures

BUDAPEST, Hungarian Academy of Sciences, Figure XIX.
CAIRO, Karaite Synagogue, Figure VI.
COPENHAGEN, The Royal Library, Figure X.
EDINBURGH, Edinburgh University Library, Figure IV.
JERUSALEM, Israel Museum, Figure V.
JERUSALEM, from private collection of Rabbi S.D. Sassoon, Figure VIII.
JERUSALEM, Schocken Institute, Figure XIII.
KREMSMÜNSTER, Benediktinerstiftsbibliothek, Figure III (Photo, Akademische Druck-u. Verlagsanstalt from the facsimile edition of *Speculum Humanae Salvationis,* Graz, 1972).
LENINGRAD, Public Library, Figure VII (Photo, V. Stassof and D. Güenzburg, *L'ornement hébreu,* Berlin, 1905, Plate III).
LONDON, Reproduced by permission of the British Library Board, Figures XI, XVI.
NEW HAVEN, François Bucher, *The Pamplona Bibles,* Yale University Press, 1970, Vol. II, Plate 98, Figure II (Photo, Charles V. Passela, New York).
NEW HAVEN, Photograph courtesy of the Yale University Art Gallery, Figure I.
OXFORD, the Curators of the Bodleian Library, Figures IX, XII, XIV.
PARMA, Biblioteca Palatina, Figure XV.
ROME, Biblioteca Apostolica Vaticana, Figure XVII.

INTRODUCTION

Ever since Muhammad spoke of the Jews as a "people of the Book," the idea has persisted that these inheritors of a sensitive and intense literary tradition have a psychic blind spot where visual receptivity is concerned. Bernard Berenson, for instance, asserted categorically that the "Jews . . . have displayed little talent for the visual, and almost none for the figurative arts. . . . To the Jews belonged the splendours and raptures of the word." The Jews, Matthew Arnold had it, excelled in the realm of ethics, not aesthetics. Sigmund Freud speculated that the biblical prohibition—the so-called "Second Commandment"—"signified subordinating sense perception to an abstract idea; it was a triumph of spirituality over the senses. . . ."

Throughout the nineteenth century when detailed catalogues of medieval Hebrew manuscripts in public European libraries were being compiled by some of the foremost Jewish scholars, they frequently supplied only brief references to, or entirely omitted any mention of, the decorations or miniatures found in these manuscripts. As a matter of fact, when Olaus Tychsen, an eighteenth-century Christian Hebraist and Orientalist, intrigued by the discovery of decorations in Hebrew manuscripts, turned to some Jewish scholars of his time for more information about these decorations, he was rudely chastised for not knowing that Judaism does not tolerate the decoration of Hebrew manuscripts. Even today prevailing scholarly opinion still holds that Judaism, constrained by an all-embracing biblical anti-iconism, has always denied the image.

If it is a fact that Judaism for psychological, biological, or spiritual reasons was unable to embrace the image, how are we to reconcile the appearance of medieval miniatures with the oft-quoted biblical injunction against the making of "any manner of likeness?" Such a reconciliation will not seem at all forced when we consider the possibility that the "Second Commandment" is not an unchanging monolithic concept in a static Jewish culture which never transcended its own particular historical context. Indeed, what we confront is a dynamic Judaism which, in the course of its three-thousand-year history, has given rise to many diverse types of life-style and expression, each with a different view of the biblical prohibition. On the one hand, we find Profiat Duran, a fifteenth-century Spanish Jewish scholar, convinced that:

> "The contemplation and study of pleasing forms, beautiful images, and drawings broadens and stimulates the mind and strengthens its faculties. . . . As with God, who wanted to beautify His Holy Place with gold, silver, jewels and precious stones, so it should be with His Holy Books" (*Ma'ase Efod,* 19).

On the other hand, in Regensburg, Germany, during that same century, Rabbi Jakob ben Moses ha-Levi Mölln strenuously objected to using the beautifully decorated prayer books handed to him for the High Holy Day synagogue services (*Sefer Maharil, Hilkhot Yom Kippur* 35b).

In short, the dogmatic insistence that Judaism has always repudiated the image does not take into account the fact that there frequently exists a wide divergence between the verbalizations of religious leaders in a particular society and the practices actually adhered to by large segments of their followers. This holds true for Christianity as well as Judaism. Saint Bernard in twelfth-century Clairvaux inveighed against "the ridiculous monsters sculpted in the cloisters"—a criticism which Rabbi Meir ben Barukh, of thirteenth-century Rothenburg, would have thought eminently reasonable. The animal and bird figures Rabbi Meir saw in contemporary Jewish prayer books did "not seem fitting . . . since when [the readers] contemplate these figures they will not incline their hearts to their Father in heaven" (*Tosafot* to Babylonian Talmud, *Yoma* 54a). We know how little St. Bernard's strictures were heeded, and we will see that Rabbi Meir's pronouncements were equally ignored.

Outright denial of the existence of figurative art among Jews is no longer as widespread as it was. Some scholars are now convinced that the suggestion first offered by Josef Strzygowski (in his *Orient oder Rom?* in 1901), that the ultimate source of many Old Testament scenes in early and medieval Christian art may be rooted in pre-existent Hellenistic Jewish illustrated manuscripts, is indeed fact. Amazing archaeological discoveries of Near Eastern remains in the twentieth century—the remarkable paintings of the third-century Dura-Europos synagogue in Syria and the figural mosaic floors of later Palestinian synagogues—have altered the once virtually uncontested scholarly faith in a rigid Jewish iconoclasm and appear to offer substantive proof for Strzygowski's brilliant surmise.

The paintings of the Dura synagogue, it has been claimed, are based on illustrated Jewish manuscript cycles, iconographic traces of which survive in later Christian and Jewish art. One unusual iconographic motif, among several, from the Dura synagogue that seems to have survived for a thousand years to reappear in

I

II

fourteenth-century Spanish Hebrew manuscripts, has been used to demonstrate the existence of ancient Jewish illustrated manuscript cycles (Figure I). It reveals the naked Egyptian princess standing in the Nile holding the child Moses in her left arm, while her three clothed maidens wait on shore. Based on a legendary elaboration of the biblical narrative (Exodus 2:5), the Dura painting has the princess herself discovering the child, rather than dispatching her slave girl to fetch the basket from the Nile waters. A fourteenth-century Spanish *Haggadah* again has the naked princess in the Nile, as at Dura, but here she has come upon the basket while two naked maidens, also in the water, stand behind her (Plate 11). The *Haggadah* scene and the Dura painting are certainly based on similar literary sources, but the immediate model of the Spanish Hebrew miniature is not the Dura painting; it is more likely the late twelfth-century Christian illustration of the same episode in the *Pamplona Bible* (Figure II).

Recent research does not seem to substantiate the assumption of manuscript sources for the Dura-Europos synagogue paintings; pattern or model books and cartoons appear to be a more plausible possibility. Unlike manuscript cycles, it should be noted, the biblical paintings at Dura follow no narrative sequential order and were not meant to enhance and explain the biblical text; rather, these paintings are bound by definite themes purposely chosen from different books of the Bible and from extra-biblical literature in order to spell out, in an analogous fashion, a liturgical-theological program of contemporary Judaism. The hypothesis of illus-

III

trated Hebrew manuscripts in classical antiquity rests largely on an *argumentum ex silentio* as no such manuscripts are known to exist. A few rabbinic sources (cf. Babylonian Talmud, *Shabbat* 103b and the earlier Hellenistic *Letter of Aristeas* 176) do speak—disparagingly—of manuscript decorations but what they address themselves to is nothing pictorial; they censure only the practice of writing in gold the *tetragrammaton* (name of God) in *Torah* scrolls.

Extra-canonical Jewish elements appearing in Christian art are also frequently cited in support of theories hypostatizing a now lost illustrated Jewish manuscript tradition in antiquity. Infrequently related to or found in Hellenistic Jewish writings or in the Septuagint, they do appear in *aggadah* and *midrash* (rabbinic legends and homiletical writings), but cannot be called upon as witnesses to lost ancient Jewish illustrated manuscript cycles, since Jewish exegetical and homiletical methods, as well as Jewish legends, were adapted by both Christian and later Muslim writers. A case in point are miniatures illustrating a Jewish legend concerning the life of Abraham. According to the legends, Abraham's search for the one God finally led to his rejection of the idol worship of his father Terah. After smashing his father's idols, Abraham was severely punished by King Nimrod who ordered the iconoclast cast into the fire of the Chaldeans, from which he was miraculously rescued. This story appears in Hebrew manuscripts of the fourteenth century (Plate 25) and is also found in coeval Christian art, the *Bible Moralisée* and the *Speculum Humanae Salvationis* manuscripts (Figure III). Usually Abraham is shown en-

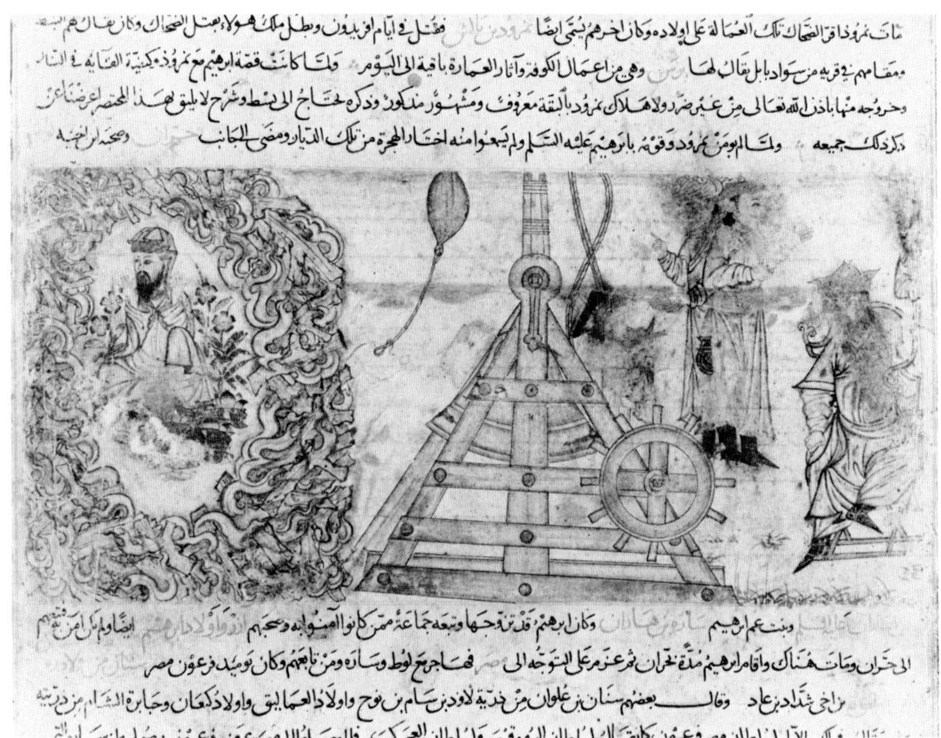

IV

gulfed by flames, with God reaching down from the ark of heaven to rescue him. Persian manuscripts of Rashid al-Din's fourteenth-century *Jāmiʿ al-Tawārīkh (Collection of Chronicles)* also illustrates this legend (Figure IV). Nimrod is surrounded by his advisers and is seated to the right of a large siege catapult, which, according to Muslim sources, Eblis (Satan) had advised building to project Abraham into the flames. On God's order, however, the fire has become cold, and Abraham sits next to a spring from which a beautiful flowerbed has sprung while the flames still engulf him.

All the images of basic Jewish legendary motifs in the three religions reveal such a rich diversity of iconography and styles as to refute the claim of a common, linear descent from lost Jewish manuscript models. They argue very strongly in favor of artistic inventiveness and originality. There is no denying, however, that the graphic evidence is indebted to a purely literary channel—folklore that Muslims and Christians freely adapted to suit their own distinctive religious traditions.

To study the illuminations in Hebrew manuscripts is to encompass at the same time much of the history of Christian and Islamic art. No unique Jewish style emerges; there is no independent medieval Jewish artistic evolution. This, of course, reflects the circumstance that Jewish history, unlike that of other continuous entities, developed and evolved primarily within multiple societies, cultures, and civilizations, and bears the imprimatur of its long, diverse, multicultural experience. A critical examination of all miniatures reveals no isolated, separate thread, but, on the contrary, a multicolored thread woven into the fabric of the Jewish involvement in the larger non-Jewish society. Thus the miniatures covering roughly eight hundred years (ca. 900 A.D.–1700 A.D.) reveal the stylistic trends prevailing in such Muslim countries as Palestine, Egypt, Yemen, and Persia under such rulers as the Fatimids, Mamluks, and Safavids. Similarly, in Christian Europe, the Hebrew miniatures from Spain, Portugal, Germany, France, and Italy evince the Romanesque, Gothic, Mudéjar, International, and Renaissance styles. No major Jewish workshops appear, as Jews were usually barred from the Christian guilds of Europe. Hence, it is not unusual to find that some of the finest Hebrew illuminations are the products of Christian ateliers. In a few cases, we do know the names of medieval Jewish artists—Joseph ha-Zarefati (Plate 10) and Joseph ibn Hayyim of Spain (Figure IX), and Joel ben Simeon of Germany and northern Italy (Plate 32). From Palma de Majorca, Spain, we have a contract of 1335 wherein Asher Bonnim Maymo undertook to copy and illuminate a Bible and two books of Maimonides for one David Isaac Cohen. Abraham ben Judah ibn Hayyim, a late fifteenth-century Portuguese Jew, even compiled a treatise in Judeo-Portuguese on the art of manuscript illumination [Parma: Bibloteca Palatina Ms. Parm. 1959 (de Rossi 945)] in the tradition of earlier Christian manuals written by Theophilus and Ceninni.

In Hebrew manuscripts the scribe was pre-eminent. He was responsible for the entire manuscript and for the initial word panels, sometimes for the decoration, and for giving directions to the artist. The vocalizer of the Hebrew text (as the Hebrew script originally had no representations of vowels) was usually also responsible for the *masorah* (lists of critical notes on the external text of the Hebrew Bible) placed at the top and bottom of the text page and in the lateral margins between the text columns. Hence, in the colophon we frequently find the name of the scribe, sometimes the name of the vocalizer, but rarely the name of the artist.

Although stylistic and decorative elements are often adapted from prevalent styles of the period and certain retrogressive tendencies are evident in manuscripts from provincial areas (especially in fifteenth-century Germany where older artistic trends had received a certain traditional authenticity and lingered on), it is in the area of paleography and iconography that distinctions arise.

Since the Hebrew script uses no capital letters, the dominance of the initial letter found in Latin Christian manuscripts could not become characteristic of Hebrew manuscripts. Instead, what developed was the use of initial word panels, although there are instances where the initial letter is employed in direct imitation of the Latin letter (Plate 32). The Hebrew letter, although it has its own obvious qualities, shows subtle changes from one country to another because the writing implements differ—calamus, a reed pen for most Oriental and *Sephardi* (Spanish-Portuguese) scribes, and a feather quill pen for most *Ashkenazi* (Franco-

V

German) and Italian scribes—and because the letter takes on some of the contours of the Arabic and Latin scripts and calligraphy. In isolated cases, as in a fifteenth-century German manuscript, we find outright imitation of the Gothic script in the Hebrew letters (*vayosh'a,* "the Lord *delivered* Israel," Exodus 14:30, Figure V).

Another distinctive feature is the use of micrography (minute script) for the *masorah* which appeared in Hebrew manuscripts of the early Muslim period and continued to be employed in Hebrew manuscripts of medieval Christian Europe. Primarily geometric or floral designs occur in the Muslim Hebrew manuscripts (Figure VI); they also assume the shapes of animal and human figures in Hebrew manuscripts of Christian Europe (Figure XI, Plate 22). These decorative games were apparently not known in *Qur'ān* manuscripts. *Carmina figurata* (poems in pictures), written so that they form representational shapes, are recorded in the Hellenistic world; Publilius Porfyrius of the fourth century A.D. wrote poems in the shape of an altar or an organ. Surviving ninth-century Aratus manuscripts (London: British Library, Ms. Harl. 647), based on earlier models, do show figures composed of a dense sequence of parallel rows of writing, all filling a specific shape, but the practice of having the letters themselves form the shape appears to be peculiar to Hebrew manuscripts.

Although many iconographic motifs have been adapted to Jewish purposes from both Christian and Islamic models, we do find eschatological, liturgical, and ceremonial scenes that belong expressly to diverse Jewish communities. Then, too, the depiction of God is scrupulously avoided, with a hand or rays usually indicating the presence of the Almighty.

The field of Hebrew illuminations is still relatively virgin territory and invites more exploration. To go from the great masterpieces of Byzantine, Celtic, and

VI

VII

Carolingian manuscript art to the field of Hebrew miniatures is at times like walking from a brilliantly lit room into one only dimly illuminated. At first, little can be perceived, but given time the observer will begin to recognize the contours of a symbolic art style—the ideographic summarizing of elements of medieval Jewry's spiritual experience.

The miniatures to be discussed will be grouped under the following rubrics:

I. Hebrew Miniature Painting from the Islamic East
  A. Egypt-Palestine, ninth–twelfth century
  B. Yemen, fifteenth century
  C. Persia, seventeenth century
II. Hebrew Miniature Painting from Western Christianity
  A. Spain-Portugal, thirteenth–fifteenth century
  B. France-Germany, thirteenth–fifteenth century
  C. Italy, thirteenth–fifteenth century

I A.) *Palestine-Egypt.* The earliest dated illuminated Hebrew manuscript comes from 895 A.D. Tiberias, Palestine. A biblical manuscript containing only the Prophets, it is a codex—a peculiarly Christian-type book which was not adopted by Jews until post-Talmudic times. The most significant and central Hebrew book for synagogal worship is, of course, the *Torah* (pentateuchal) scroll—a book never illuminated and retaining its scroll format to this very day. No Hebrew illuminated manuscripts are known from the Byzantine or Sasanian Empires; only some figural Byzantine synagogal floor mosaics have survived. The 895 A.D. codex belongs to a group of Bibles produced in Palestine and Egypt between the ninth and twelfth centuries. Some of these manuscripts have carpet pages preceding the biblical text, as do opening pages of *Qur'ān* manuscripts. Most of these Bibles were written for Karaites, a schismatic Jewish movement that originated in the eighth-century Abbasid East and stressed asceticism and messianism. The Karaites had elevated the authority of the Bible and rejected the Rabbinism which owed its authority to the *Talmud.* The style and motifs of these Hebrew manuscripts share many features in common with contemporary *Qur'ān* manuscripts—the abstract, geometric patterns and motifs with vegetal and floral suggestions, especially the palmette *ansa* attached to the outer design of the carpet page. Even the size is similar to *Qur'āns* donated to mosques. A typical page using only gold and blue paint shows text and decoration well integrated (Figure VI). Between an inner and an outer circle of small blue dots and gold is an open gold rosette composed of scroll work and leaves. The large gold circle is framed by a double band of writing. Inside are twenty-three small circles of figured text, each with a gold dot in the center. In four corners are mandorlas of writing. Four pointed micrographic mandorlas with arrow-shaped heads point compasslike to micrographic bands, which in turn are flanked by gold palmettes and a tiny diamond shape with eight projecting petals. Stylistically related is a page from the *Leningrad Bible,* dated 929 and made perhaps in Palestine or Egypt (Figure VII). The carpet page, again, has such decorations as interlacing foliage scrolls and stylized palmette *ansas* on the exterior frame; it also has a schematic rendering of the Tabernacle and its vessels. A square, seven-branched lampstand dominates the center; above it is the ark of the covenant flanked by two stylized leaves, perhaps symbolic of the cherubim. The two rectangular tablets within the ark are topped by a reversed trapezoid—reminiscent of writing tablets. To the side are such implements as the jar of *manna,* an altar, and Aaron's flowering rod. The Karaites likened their Bibles to the wilderness Tabernacle *(ohel mo'ed);* the *ohel* was a metaphor for Scripture and hence is probably illustrated here, as well as in a related fragmentary page. These Tabernacle depictions have often been confused with the Messianic Temple appearing in later Spanish Hebrew manuscripts (Plates 6–9), but there is no direct relation between these two conceptions, nor are they linked, as is often claimed, with earlier synagogue mosaics which clearly show the *Torah* ark (not the Temple or the Tabernacle), flanked by symbols of the Jewish holidays. Most of the carpet pages and decorations in Hebrew manuscripts from Muslim Egypt and Palestine served to embellish Bibles, although some of the manuscripts are adorned children's textbooks, ornamental marriage contracts *(ketubbot),* and liturgical and scientific books. These all display the geometric, abstract ornamentation found in contemporary Islamic manuscripts.

IB.) *Yemen.* From remote fifteenth-century Yemen some biblical manuscripts with carpet pages have survived, probably the work of Jewish artist-scribes. The decorations and colors were perhaps inspired by enamel glass objects and designs on metal work. Scribes and illuminators skillfully combined artistic features of

Mamluk Far Eastern and Jewish derivation. The use of biblical micrography to form animal objects constituted a departure from the strictly floral and geometric forms of Masoretic micrography in earlier Muslim Hebrew manuscripts (Plates 1–2).

IC.) *Persia.* The only Muslim figural decorations in Hebrew manuscripts come from seventeenth-century Persia. These are Judeo-Persian manuscript copies of the biblical epics written by the Persian Jewish poets Maulānā Šāhīn of the fourteenth century, and Imrānī of the sixteenth. Elaborately illuminated, these seventeenth-century manuscripts are intricately connected, both in their iconography and their style, to Safavid provincial styles and iconography—dependent upon, or influenced by the styles of Isfahan (Plates 3–4).

IIA.) *Spain-Portugal.* The Islamic artistic traditions were continued in Spain where, under the Umayyad Caliphate and the successor Emirates, Jews rose to high court positions. Unfortunately, no illuminated Hebrew manuscripts have survived from the tenth and eleventh centuries, which have been termed the first Golden Age for Jews in Muslim Spain. Hebrew miniatures did not appear in Spain until the thirteenth century, when Jews experienced their second Golden Age, this time in Christian Spain. Inheriting knowledge of the complex urban economy Islam had developed in Spain, Jews were invited to serve Spanish Christian rulers in such key positions as tax farmers, bailiffs, counsellors, and physicians during the thirteenth and fourteenth centuries. A privileged Jewish aristocracy arose, accepted as equal in court circles and able to avail itself of the highest cultural and artistic attainments of Christian Spain. In Christian Spain, the artistic traditions of Gothic Europe and Mudéjar (the Islamic styles) continued to exist side by side, as discernible in Hebrew manuscripts. The earliest Hebrew illuminations came from such flourishing Jewish centers as Toledo and Burgos (Plate 5). These were Bible manuscripts, and date from the thirteenth century. Some ten manuscripts are extant from Toledo with arabesque carpet pages that precede and follow the biblical text, enclosing it, as it were, like a binding. The models for these decorations were probably Muslim decorations found on buildings and in manuscripts. A page from the richly illuminated *Farhi Bible* again testifies to the survival of the Islamic tradition in Hebrew manuscripts (Figure VIII). Written by the aristocrat Elisha ben Abraham ben Beveniste ben Elisha Crescas in the Catalonian region between 1366–1382, the manuscript's twenty-nine preliminary carpet pages are often framed with acanthus leaves—common to French Gothic—attached to two corners. The gold Hebrew verse is from Proverbs 3:17–18: ". . . all her paths are peace. She is a tree of life to those who lay hold of her; and those who hold her fast. . . ." The basic design develops from the patterns of two overlapping squares within a circle. This core is transformed into a complex design of white intersecting ribbons set against a textured background. The roundel in turn forms a contrast to the floral pattern

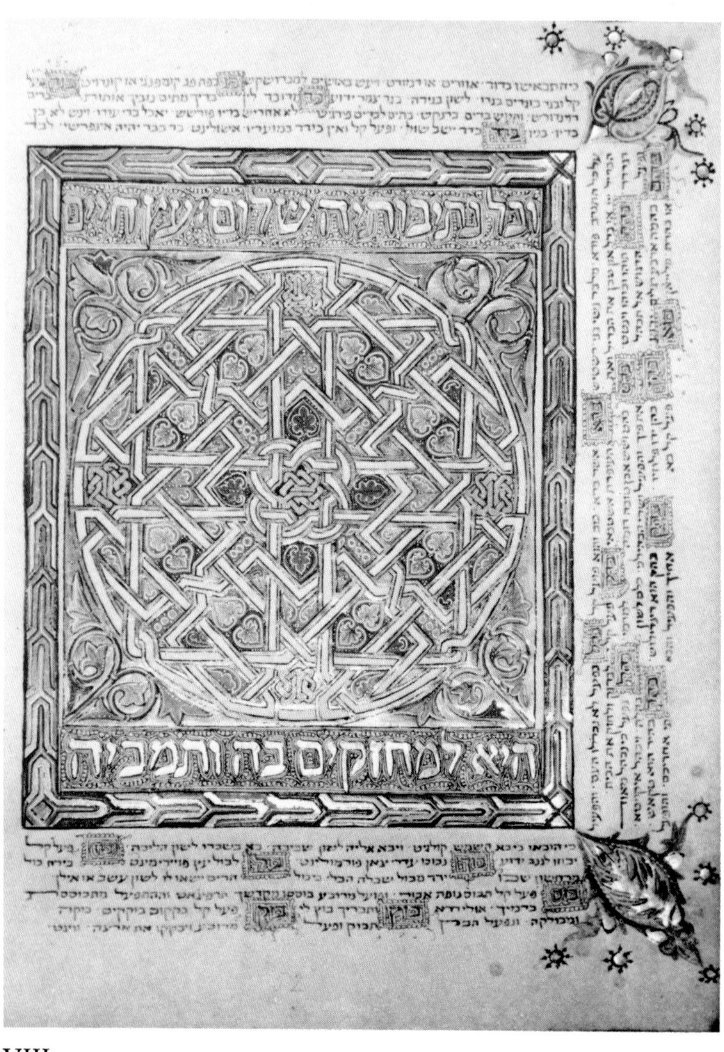

VIII

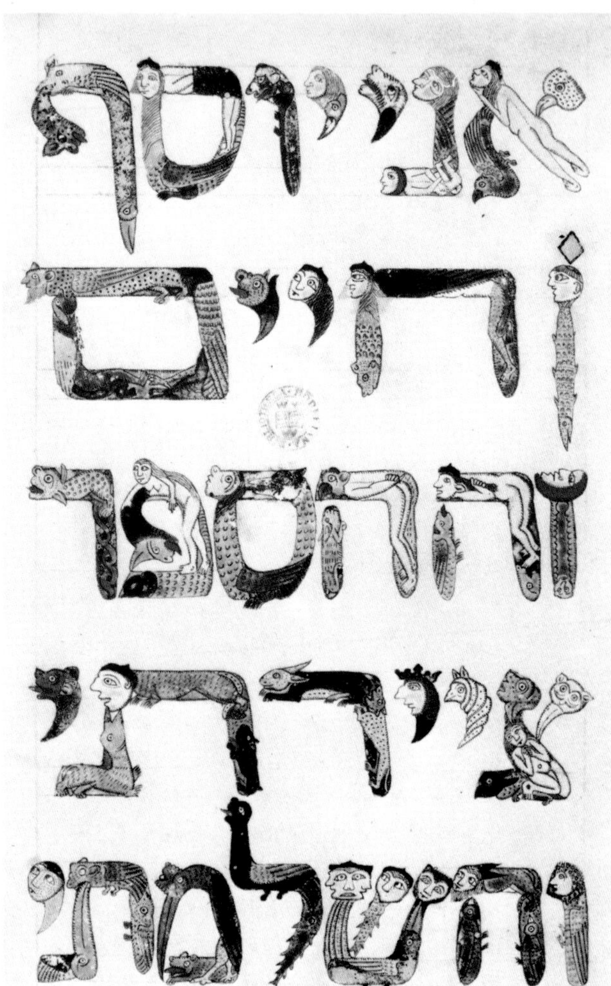

IX

in the four corners. We need only examine a decorative page in a *Qur'ān* from Valencia, Spain, 1182 (Istanbul: University Library, Ms. A 6754, fol. 1v) to find a similar color pattern and design. Stucco work, tiles and wood-carved Mudéjar art and manuscripts contain decorations similar to those in the *Farhi* carpet pages.

The *Farhi Bible* is part of a unique iconographic development in Spanish Hebrew Bibles, which began in the late thirteenth century and to which some twenty surviving illuminated Bible manuscripts offer testimony. A common designation for the Hebrew Bible was "twenty-four," alluding to the twenty-four books of the Hebrew Bible. From the fourteenth century on in Spain, it became customary to call the Bible *mikdashyah* (Sanctuary of God). The traditional three-fold division of the twenty-four books—*Torah* (Pentateuch)–Prophets–Writings (Hagiographa)—was likened to the three divisions of the ancient Solomonic Temple. Moreover, usually on the preliminary folios preceding the biblical text, it became customary to depict the gold and silver cult implements which, according to rabbinic tradition, had stood in the Temple of Solomon—though such illustrations are not found embellishing the descriptive passages of the cult vessels in Exodus and Leviticus (Plates 6–7). Most of the cult vessels in these Spanish Hebrew manuscripts are cited in the Bible; others are found in the *Mishneh Torah,* the legal code of the most influential and most widely read twelfth-century Spanish Jewish philosopher, Maimonides. According to Maimonides, all the depicted cult vessels existed in the Solomonic Temple, which a King-Messiah would rebuild in the messianic future. Further underscoring the association of the cultic implements with the future Temple is the introduction—in the second quarter of the fourteenth century—of distinct iconographic variants on the basic theme: musical instruments which the Levites used in the Temple service appeared, and a diminutive Mount of Olives is depicted amidst the Sanctuary vessels (Plates 8–9). Again, Spanish commentators like David Kimhi asserted that the righteous dead would be resurrected on the Mount of Olives in the Land of Israel, after having arrived there by means of underground caverns, to behold the splendors of the Messianic Temple.

When the Spanish Jew included representations of the Sanctuary utensils on the opening folios of his Bible, he was giving visual expression to the ardent hope which Don Samuel ha-Levi Abulafia, chief treasurer of King Pedro I of Castile, inscribed on his synagogue's eastern wall (El Tránsito, Toledo, ca. 1357): that "he might be deemed worthy to behold the rebuilding of the Temple so that he and his sons might forever serve the Lord." The artistic models for some of the Temple implements appear to be rooted in Islamic ceramic and metal vessels.

Within two Hebrew Bibles we also find the survival of ninth–eleventh century Mozarabic artistic traditions, especially in the zoomorphic decoration of the imaginative Hebrew signature of the artist of the 1300 *Cervera Bible* (Plate 10). It is most unusual to find the signature of a medieval Jewish artist in a Hebrew manuscript. What is even more astounding is that this manuscript found its way to La Coruña in northwestern Spain and served as the model for the so-called *Kennicott Bible,* prepared for Isaac ben Solomon de Braga in July 1476, by the scribe Moses ben Jacob ibn Zabara, and the artist Joseph ibn Hayyim (Figure IX). The zoomorphic colophon, in its decorative and figural schemes, manifests striking similarities to the *Cervera Bible,* but Joseph ibn Hayyim did not simply copy; he assimilated his models creatively. He introduced new motifs and transposed into the *Kennicott Bible* designs first known to him as elements in contemporary playing cards or from related graphic sources.

The most important illuminated Jewish book introduced in Christian Spain was undoubtedly the Passover *Haggadah,* meant for home observance. The *Haggadah* is a collection of biblical and homiletical verses, poems, and religious customs and songs, focusing essentially on the Exodus of the ancient Hebrews, their attainment of freedom from Egyptian bondage, and their ultimate hope of redemption with the coming of Elijah, the messianic herald. The *Haggadah* (literally *the telling*) is recited in traditional Jewish homes during the service known as the *Seder* (literally *order* of ceremonial) on the first two Passover eves. A product of the rabbinic mind, the *Haggadah* was originally a part of the prayer codices and apparently not illuminated. The main body of the text had become established in ninth century (A.D.) Babylonia. The earliest independent illuminated *Haggadah* manuscripts probably date from thirteenth-century Western Europe. From Spain some fifteen illuminated *Haggadah* manuscripts have survived, mostly from the fourteenth century. They clearly reveal the French High Gothic and Italian Gothic styles of the period. The manuscripts feature illustrations of the ritual and textual aspects of the *Haggadah* text proper. They are usually prefaced with full-page nontextual miniatures from the book of Exodus (although some manuscripts begin with illustrations from Genesis) and have appended to them a collection of *piyyutim* (liturgical poems) (Plates 11–16). The stylistic influences on these *Haggadah* manuscripts, their regional variations, and dating still require investigation.

The rise of private, liturgical Hebrew books, such as the *Haggadah,* is not surprising, since by the thirteenth century monasteries no longer had a monopoly on book production. The social and economic growth of town life in Europe, the rise of universities, and the emergence of a new burgher class spurred an increasing demand for private Christian illuminated books as well, a demand met by lay artists in the newly established craft guilds. Especially favored were luxurious copies of Latin Psalters in twelfth- and thirteenth-century France and England. Frequently appended to these private Psalters were, among others, pictorial Old Testament prefaces. Just as the Old Testament pictorial introduction in the Psalter related to the canonical hours and made explicit that which was implicit in the Psalms, so did the *Haggadah's* biblical cycle make explicit that which was implicit in the *Haggadah* text. Although in style, decoration, and format the *Haggadah* often parallels contemporary Christian manuscripts, such as the Psalter, the *Haggadah* itself, as a literary expression, has no counterpart among medieval Christian ritual books.

Another important illuminated manuscript for the Spanish Jews was the *Moreh Nevukhim (Guide to the Perplexed)*—a philosophical work by Maimonides which tried to reconcile Jewish tradition with Aristotle. Maimonides's clothing of Judaism in Aristotelian garb formed a philosophical bridge for the Jewish aristocracy and allowed them to function at court (where Greek philosophical thinking was fashionable), without relinquishing their Judaism. Many of the manuscripts possess elaborate textual ornamentation, but few contain textual illustrations. A manuscript, made in 1348 Barcelona, reveals the style of the Italian *trecento,* especially of the Bolognese school. Its similarity in style and iconography has permitted the attribution of a group of Latin Catalonian manuscripts to the mid-fourteenth-century so-called "Master of Saint Mark." One page (the Introduction to Part II, dealing with the philosophical propositions to prove the existence of God) may portray Aristotle seated upon a throne explaining his theory of the creation of the universe to his five pupils. In his lap rests an open book, while in his uplifted hand he holds an astrolabe; the sun and moon are visible above, in the half-arc of heaven (Figure X).

X

XI

The violent destruction of Jewish communities in Spain in 1391 and the final expulsion of Jews in 1492 wrote *finis* to some of the important centers of illuminated Hebrew manuscript production.

The last school of Hebrew book painting in the Iberian peninsula flourished in Lisbon, Portugal, in the last quarter of the fifteenth century. Most of the manuscripts produced here, prior to the Jewish expulsion in 1496–1497, were Bibles (Plate 40). These manuscripts have wide decorated border frames on the opening page of each biblical book, as well as embellishments of the appended pages of the grammatical treatises and those dealing with the Masoretic variations of the two Masoretic schools. No text illustrations are found.

IIB.) *France-Germany.* Although Jews had participated as merchants furthering commerce and a money economy in old established, as well as newly emerging, towns in Germany and northern France since the tenth century, and had functioned as money lenders from the twelfth century onward, no illuminated manuscripts from the early period of their involvement there have survived. The earliest extant manuscript is a two-volume Rashi commentary to the Bible made in the region of Würzburg, Germany, in 1233 (Plate 17). In the eleventh century, Rashi of Troyes in northeastern France wrote a literal exposition of Scripture which greatly influenced contemporary Christian exegesis, such as that of the Victorines. The Würzburg manuscript's seventeen miniatures, mainly of the Book of Genesis, are all appropriately placed in initial word panels to introduce the pericope *(parashah)* of the week. They reflect the late Romanesque style current in south Germany. No other extant manuscript of Rashi's commentary of the Bible has so elaborate a cycle of biblical illuminations; most others have simply decorative motifs. This cycle, it should be noted, bears no stylistic or iconographic relationship to earlier Jewish art, but is rooted in contemporary German art. *The Sacrifice of Isaac* (fol. 18v) is a good example. As in the Sacrifice sculpted on the chancel side relief of the Marienkirche of Wechselburg, ca. 1235, we see a nude Isaac seated upon the altar, hands tied, while an angel arrests Abraham's uplifted weapon. No longer is Isaac clothed, lying on the altar with the hand of God intervening, as in the third-century Dura-Europos synagogue mural.

The Bible itself, frequently in bold, square *Ashkenazi* script and on large folios, was also illuminated. Several south German Bibles from the thirteenth and fourteenth centuries have come down to us (cf. Milan: Biblioteca Ambrosiana, B. 30–32 Inf. and Parma: Biblioteca Palatina, Mss. Parm. 3286–87). Unlike most of the Spanish Hebrew Bibles, these manuscripts sometimes do contain illustrations of biblical events within the text. A smaller Bible (Plate 18) from the early fourteenth century has forty-six roundels with biblical scenes surrounding the initial word panel of Genesis. Painted in blue and red, they follow a similar format found in *Bible Moralisée* manuscripts and, of course, in stained glass windows. Also from the early fourteenth century comes a Pentateuch whose full-page illuminations belong to a group of Hebrew and Latin manuscripts illuminated in a south German workshop (Plate 19).

Undoubtedly the richest Hebrew biblical illuminations from the *Ashkenazi* (Franco-German) region are found in a Miscellany, most of whose illuminations, painted in northeastern France, date from the last quarter of the thirteenth century. Some forty-one biblical miniatures include scenes from the lives of Adam and Eve, Noah, Abraham, Moses, Aaron, Samson, David, Solomon, Daniel, Esther, and even from the apocryphal Book of Judith (reclaimed by Jews in the Middle Ages), as well as some eschatological subjects. Painted by several clearly distinguishable hands, its elegant style is closely related to the most advanced High Gothic found in the schools of Paris (Plates 20–21).

The Islamic Hebrew tradition of micrography continued, especially in German Hebrew Bible manuscripts. The Masoretic notes, however, were no longer devoted exclusively to geometric and vegetal forms, but showed imaginative innovations of animal grotesqueries as well as human beings (Plate 22). In a few cases, we even have textual illustrations, such as a ram in the thicket next to the Binding of Isaac story, and a bearded, praying Jonah swallowed by the "huge fish" of which the Hebrew text speaks (Figure XI).

XII

The earliest illuminated manuscript of a *Mishneh Torah,* Maimonides's legal code was written in 1295–96, perhaps at Cologne, Germany. The style of the marginal paintings and decorations is, however, related to a group of manuscripts from late thirteenth- and early fourteenth-century Cambrai in Flanders (Plate 23).

No doubt, the most important manuscript illuminations in *Ashkenazi* communities are those of the *mahzor* (literally *cycle*)—a book containing the complete prayers and *piyyutim* (liturgical poetic insertions) for the seven special Sabbaths and all of the holidays. No elaborately painted *Sephardi mahzorim* are known. Huge in format and written in clear, monumental *Ashkenazi* script, the illuminated *Ashkenazi mahzor* came into being in the second half of the thirteenth century. The wide selection of *piyyutim* to be sung by the *hazzan* (cantor) and the great weight and size of the book indicate that these thirteenth–fourteenth century *mahzorim* were probably not intended for individuals, but for the synagogue. The *mahzor* was in some ways, of course, a counterpart to the Breviary—the devotional book used primarily by the Roman Catholic clergy, its format established in the thirteenth century and its large size meant for the Gothic lectern. As a matter of fact, an inscription in one *mahzor* calls it a *Breviarium Judaicum*. Three *mahzorim* probably date from the second half of the thirteenth century and were made in the Rhineland or in southern Germany (*Worms Mahzor,* Jerusalem: Hebrew National and University Library, Ms. Hebr. 4°781; Oxford: Bodleian Library, Mss. Laud. Or. 321 and Mich. 617 and 627). The most extensive cycle of illuminations with initial word panels and marginal paintings is in the *Leipzig Mahzor,* probably created in the Upper Rhineland around Lake Constance between 1320–1330 (Plates 24–26).

XIII

A special iconography developed for the *mahzor,* such as the red heifer set next to the liturgical reading for *Shabbat Parah* (pericope Heifer); a scale for weighing the shekels painted next to *Shabbat Shekalim* (pericope Scales); signs of the zodiac and labors of the months next to the *piyyut* praying for dew, recited on the first day of Passover; an open gate next to the morning service *piyyut* for the Day of Atonement, "He who opens the Gates of Mercy;" or roses next to the *musaf* (additional) service *piyyut* on *Yom Kippur* (Day of Atonement), "Rose of the valley." The most significant image in the *mahzor* for the *Rosh ha-Shanah* (New Year) service was the *Akedat Yitzhak* (Binding of Isaac). Rabbinic tradition saw in the *Akedat* an instrument of vicarious atonement whereby God forgives the

XIV

sins of the Jews because of the merit of their ancestors Abraham and Isaac. In a fourteenth-century German *mahzor,* the initial word panel carries the word *melekh* ("O *King,* girt with power . . ."), of the *piyyut* recited in the morning service of the first day of *Rosh ha-Shanah.* The pen drawings have Isaac kneeling upon a draped altar; Abraham, holding the knife in his right hand, indicates Isaac with his left; a winged angel in the upper left-hand corner points to Abraham and the ram in the center. In the upper right-hand corner, a man is blowing the *shofar* (ram's horn)—alluding thereby to the belief that Isaac's sacrificial binding had occurred on *Rosh ha-Shanah.* Acanthus tendrils, rosette borders, and grotesqueries with leaves in their mouths, drawn with red and sepia ink, are similar to Upper Rhenish Latin illuminations of the fourteenth century (Figure XII).

A German *mahzor* of the fourteenth century, along with the *Leipzig Mahzor* and other manuscripts stemming from southern Germany, display a unique characteristic: the depiction of human figures with animal and bird heads (Plates 27–28). Of course, in Christian art, the four Evangelists are frequently shown with human bodies and the heads of their respective symbolic animals; Saint Christopher is sometimes depicted dog-headed, as are people on the tympanum of the church of La Madeleine, Vézelay. Several theories have emerged to explain the avoidance of the human face in the German Jewish manuscripts. Most scholars feel that it is attributable to an iconophobic tendency in contemporary German Jewry; one scholar claims that these characteristics are caricatures traceable to the medieval stage; others are convinced that they represented godly grace—elevation above the human. None of these theories is satisfactory, since the evidence of the miniatures contradicts the various hypotheses. In the mystical literature of the circle that gathered around the twelfth-century Judah he-Hasid (Judah, the Pious), we do find mention of dog-headed and bird-beaked human beings. The whole problem needs further study.

The luxurious and creative quality of the earlier German Hebrew books is generally missing in fifteenth-century manuscripts (Plate 29). No longer wealthy merchants or money lenders, Jews had by then been reduced to peddling and making small loans and were subjected to mounting persecutions and martyrdom. Not only the art, but the literature of the period, reveals little creative spark. A Miscellany from the Middle Rhine region is a good example of German illustrations of this period, introducing entirely new iconographic themes which deal with messianic speculations and martyrdom (Plates 30–31).

The book most frequently illustrated during the fifteenth century is the Passover *Haggadah*. The cycle of illustrations in several German *Haggadah* manuscripts of the second half of the fifteenth century consists of marginal illustrations conveying ceremonial, textual, biblical, and eschatological aspects of the *Seder* liturgy. Stressing folklore and humor, the linear depictions sketched in outline and filled with color are realistic and naive, and show the impact of new graphic techniques like the woodcut. In its marginal illustrations, the German *Haggadah* follows a tradition established by the earlier so-called monastic Byzantine Psalters of the eleventh and twelfth centuries. Frequently, we find folk rhymes accompanying the figures—a practice popular also in French and German Christian illustrations of the period. In the *Nuremberg Haggadah,* for instance, we see a family gathered around a table, decorating the *matzot* (unleavened bread); below two people are busy baking the *matzot* in an oven, behind which two boys are hiding (Figure XIII). The flying streamer above the boys reads: "In secret before the *Seder* the *matzot* they ate, like bridegrooms consummating vows before the marriage fête." A man near the oven points to the boys: "Look and view the thief, the *matzah* is still between his teeth." Legendary biblical motifs such as Pharaoh bathing in the blood of Jewish children and Zipporah nourishing Moses in prison also abound. Many *Haggadah* illustrations interpret the text playfully, yet literally; in drawings accompanying the words, "You open (the conversation) for him," a man pries open with both his hands the mouth of the simple son (who, according to the *Haggadah* text, does not know how to ask questions). Next to the words, "this bitter herb (*maror*)," a man is often seen pointing to his wife as he holds up the *maror*. Several manuscripts entitled *Meshal ha-Kadmoni (Fable of the Easterner),* written by the thirteenth-century Spanish poet and physician, Isaac ben Solomon ibn Abi Sahula, were popular in southern Germany and northern Italy and were frequently given extensive illustrations in the second half of the fifteenth century. Sahula's work consists of allegories in rhymed prose, many in the form of animal fables. One of the earliest manuscripts of this book is dated 1450; in style it is closely related to an illustrated *mahzor* made between 1450–53 in Ulm and Treviso [Parma: Biblioteca

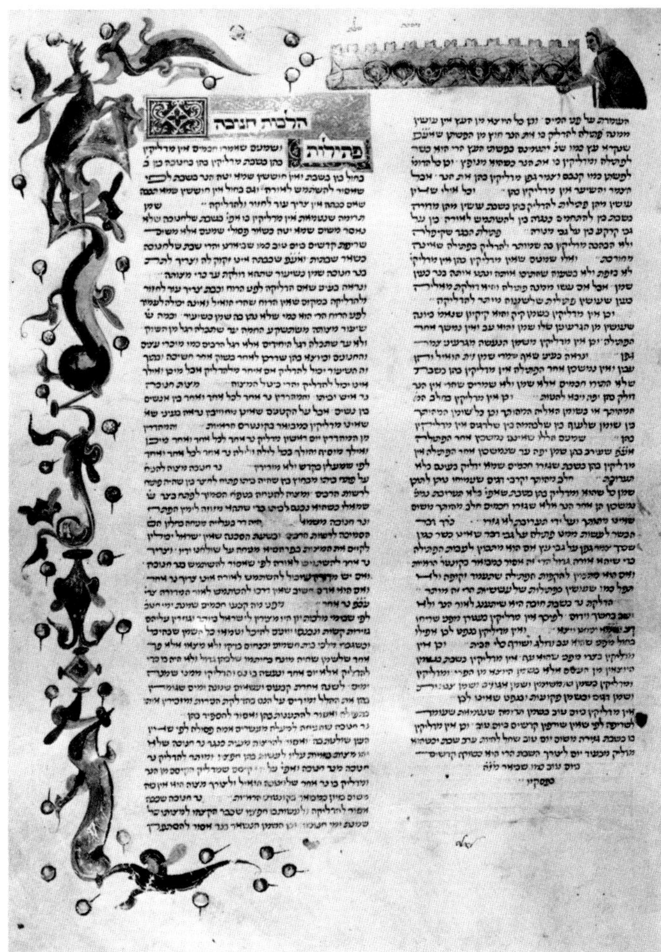

XV

XVI

Palatina, Ms. Parm. 2895 (de Rossi 653)] (Figure XIV). One typical page shows a lion, a fox, and a buck drawn in a manner reminiscent of woodcuts. The inscription reads: "The form of the lion is before him, known and familiar."

IIC.) *Italy.* Jews were invited to participate actively in the development of the mercantile city states of Italy, from the thirteenth century onward, as loan bankers. Many illustrated manuscripts have survived from this experience, but study of their miniatures presents difficulties. Many have been inadequately researched, or even published. Furthermore, the persecutions Jews suffered in such countries as Germany and Spain brought to Italy many refugees who, at times, carried on their previous scribal, artistic and iconographic traditions. This is true of some fifteenth-century *Ashkenazi Haggadah* manuscripts, especially those linked with the artist Joel ben Simeon (Plate 32). The illuminations of some Italian Hebrew manuscripts were done by the finest artists working in Italy. Also notable was the introduction of new iconographic themes and new books chosen for illustration.

The earliest illuminations in Italy appear to have come from the Rome region toward the end of the thirteenth century. Many of these manuscripts are Bibles with initial word panel decorations and marginal ornamentations. The earliest dated one

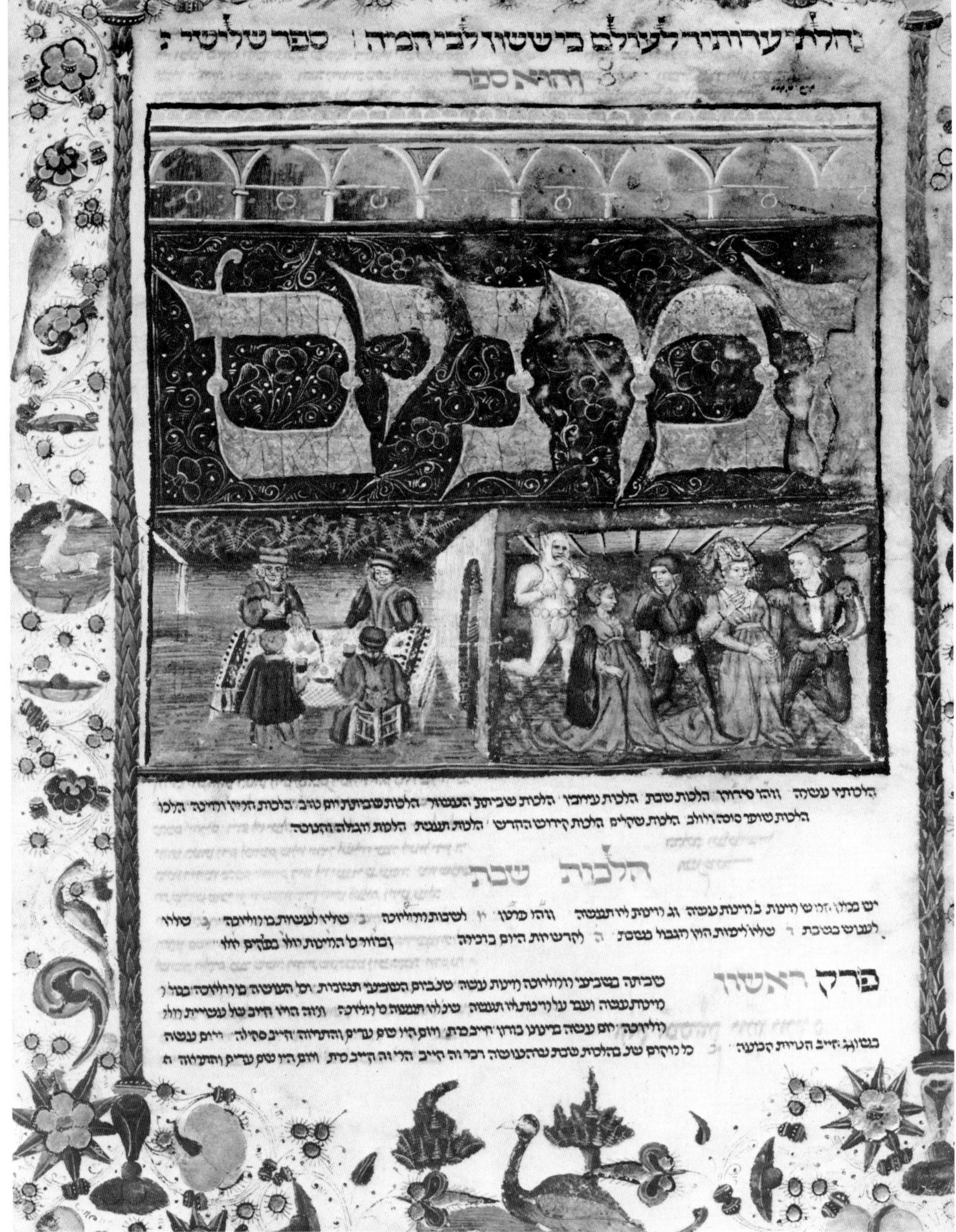
הלכות שבת

פרק ראשון

XVII

appears to have been made in 1284 in Rome (Cambridge: Emmanuel College, Ms. I.I. 5–7). An unusual manuscript is a Hebrew Psalter from this period. Decorative word panels and marginal illustrations introduce each Psalm; some Psalms have textual illustrations. The Christian Psalter, of course, enjoyed great popularity from the eighth to the fourteenth centuries. In Hebrew manuscripts it was usually not treated as a separate book, nor was it extensively illuminated. A typical page of our Hebrew Psalter with commentary by Abraham ibn Ezra depicts the marginal illustration to Psalm 137 (numbered Psalm 138): "By the waters of Babylon, there we sat down and wept when we remembered Zion. On the willows there we hung our lyres" (Figure XV). Two agitated figures in sharp outline and vibrant colors, one baring his bosom, the other drying his tears, are seen above the schematically drawn water. Initial word panels, rich leafy tendrils framing the text on two sides out of which grow stocky human torsos, are similar to decorations from the Emilian region.

The contribution of Bologna to the history of miniature painting from the thirteenth century onward was the illustration of legal texts. This practice may have exerted some influence on Hebrew books, since we find a number of illuminated Hebrew legal works dating from the fourteenth century. The *halakhic* (legal) decisions of the Italian Talmudist Rabbi Isaiah of Trani the Younger, copied at Bologna in 1347, is a good example. The text illustrating the laws of *Hanukkah* (mid-winter Feast of Dedication) shows a man kindling the wicks of the eight oil spouts on the burners of the bench-type lamp (Figure XVI). The richly foliated borders are illuminated with gold dots and a stag, and may stem from the workshop of Niccolo di Giacomo da Bologna, the most productive workshop of the second half of the fourteenth century. Another legal codex, the *Mishneh Torah* of Maimonides (Jerusalem: Hebrew National and University Library, Ms. Hebr. 4°1193) was copied in Spain or southern France and brought to Italy at the end of the fourteenth century where it was undoubtedly illuminated in the atelier of Matteo di Ser Cambio. Unlike those of the *Mishneh Torah* copied in Germany in 1295–96 (Plate 23), these miniatures deal with definite concepts of Jewish law and custom. The section dealing with the prohibition of idolatry, for example, has a marginal illustration at the bottom of the page within a floral medallion, which shows the offender being pushed into the stoning pit. The fleshy, curling leaves, the geometrical interlacings, the delicate handling of colors and figures, disclose a close affinity to Matteo di Ser Cambio's *Statute and Register of the Money Changer's Guild in Perugia* (Perugia: Collegio del Cambio, Ms. I, fol. 3).

Without question, the most splendid Hebrew manuscripts came from Renaissance Italy, where Jews participated in such learned humanist circles as those associated with Pico della Mirandola. Affluent Jewish loan bankers, such as the Da Pisa and Norsa families, probably imitated the fashionable pasttime of the Medici and Este families in commissioning both liturgical and secular books, often in Hebrew translation, for their private libraries.

A beautiful legal codex, written at Mantua in 1435, is the *Arba'ah Turim* of Jacob ben Asher, a German codifier who lived in fourteenth-century Toledo, Spain. Its elegant swaying figures and decorations reveal the courtly International Gothic Lombard style (Plates 33–34). Also from Lombardy is a two-volume *Mishneh Torah* from the third quarter of the fifteenth century. The first volume—long thought lost—is in the Vatican Library. The Hebrew letters, *zemanim* (Seasons), with a bold, chiseled quality, introduce the third book of Maimonides's code dealing with the Sabbath and holidays (Figure XVII). The border is surrounded by delicate floral and animal decorations. On the left, below the letters, we see four men around a table holding cups of wine—an allusion to the autumnal *Sukkot* (Tabernacles) celebration. To the right, in the interior of a house two couples are dancing while a jester prances behind them—perhaps referring to the celebration of *Purim.* A typical page from the second volume once again reveals the same title panel—this time the fourteenth book of Maimonides, *shoftim* (Judges), which deals with capital punishment, testimony, war, etc. (Figure XVIII). On top, set within a deep landscape are two jousting knights—alluding to warfare. Below the handsome letters we see another outdoor scene. In front of a wattled fence, two witnesses bring the accused to face four judges seated upon a bench. The stocky figures with their sculpturally modeled garments show, in the second volume, a different and more accomplished hand from that responsible for the first volume.

Secular manuscripts such as the famous medical *Canon of Medicine* by Avicenna (Plate 35) and the *Book of Principles (Sefer ha-Ikkarim)* of Joseph Albo, a Spanish preacher and philosopher, are also introduced (Plate 36). They reveal the hands of many Renaissance artists who worked for Jews as well as non-Jews. The Avicenna *Canon* may betray the imprint of the ateliers of Leonardo da Besozzo and Cristoforo Cortese, just as the Albo text shows the influence of the "Uccelesque Master" and follows the practice of humanistic books with white vine interlaces in the margins of the manuscripts. Influences such as those of Zenobi Strozzi [Parma: Biblioteca Palatina, Ms. Parm. 3236 (de Rossi 490)] and Attavante (Rome: Biblioteca Casanatense, Ms. Ebr. 2830) are also visible in Hebrew manuscripts.

By far the richest manuscript from Renaissance Italy is a Miscellany with over three-hundred text illustrations—the so-called *Rothschild Miscellany.* This manuscript, undoubtedly made for a rich Jewish loan banker, merits further study (Plates 37–38). A Bible from the late fifteenth century reflects the peculiar fate of many Hebrew books. This Bible manuscript had been begun in Portugal (Plate 40), but was brought to Italy. Those pages illuminated in Italy show the revival of antique motifs so popular in northern Italy (Plate 39).

Also popular in Italy were small Hebrew prayer books, not too different in format from the diminutive Christian Book of Hours and the pocket size Bibles, already known in thirteenth-century France. A prayer book made at Pesaro in 1481 contains marginal illustrations dealing with the Jewish holidays and life-cycle

XVIII

ceremonies. The large open flowers, the filigree ornament background, and the framed panels of animals are standard features of Ferrarese work of this period (Figure XIX) (cf. a manuscript made in Pesaro 1480, formerly Sassoon Collection, Ms. 23).

Just as was true of Christian manuscripts, Hebrew manuscripts reached their artistic heights in Renaissance Italy. Gradually, however, they came to be replaced by the printed book.

In sum, Hebrew illuminated books refract the multifaceted involvement of Jews in major cultures of the Christian West and the Islamic East. Adapting the major artistic styles of these civilizations, they conveyed their own unique religious traditions and responded to their own religious imperatives.

Our short survey obviously cannot do justice to all aspects of an area of research badly in need of more exploration; it can only skim the surface in the hope of opening doors for others to pass through.

XIX

SELECTED BIBLIOGRAPHY

Ameisenowa, Z. "Die hebräische Sammelhandschrift Add. 11639 des British Museum," *Wiener Jahrbuch für Kunstgeschichte* 24 (1971): 10–48.

———. "Animal-Headed Gods, Evangelists, Saints and Righteous Men," *Journal of the Warburg and Courtauld Institutes* 12 (1949): 21–45.

Antonioli Martelli, V. and Mortara Ottolenghi, L. *Manoscritti biblici ebraici decorati.* Catalogue of Exhibition at Biblioteca Trivulziana, Castello Sforzesco. Milan, 1966.

Avrin, L. R. K. "The Illuminations in the Moshe ben-Asher Codex of 895 C.E." Unpublished Ph.D. dissertation, University of Michigan, 1974.

Beit-Arié, M. *Hebrew Codicology.* Paris, 1977.

———. "Joel ben Simeon's Manuscripts: A Codicologer's View," *Journal of Jewish Art* 3/4 (1977): 25–39.

Blondheim, D. S. "An Old Portuguese Work on Manuscript Illumination," *Jewish Quarterly Review* 19 (1928): 97–135; 20 (1929): 283–284.

Edmunds, S. "A Note on the Art of Joseph ibn Hayyim," *Studies in Bibliography and Booklore* 11 (1976): 25–40.

Ettinghausen, R. "Yemenite Bible Manuscripts of the XVth Century," *Eretz-Israel* 7 (1964): 32*–39* and in Gutmann, *No Graven Images,* 429–465.

Ferber, S. "Micrography: A Jewish Art Form," *Journal of Jewish Art* 3/4 (1977): 12–24.

Gutmann, J. "The Haggadic Motif in Jewish Iconography," *Eretz-Israel* 6 (1960): 16*–22*.

———. "The Illuminated Medieval Passover Haggadah: Investigations and Research Problems," *Studies in Bibliography and Booklore* 7 (1965): 3–25.

———. "Judeo-Persian Miniatures," *Studies in Bibliography and Booklore* 8 (1968): 54–76 and *No Graven Images,* 466–488.

———. "Thirteen Manuscripts in Search of an Author: Joel ben Simeon, 15th-Century Scribe-Artist," *Studies in Bibliography and Booklore* 9 (1970): 76–95.

———, ed. *No Graven Images: Studies in Art and the Hebrew Bible.* New York, 1971.

———; Knaus, H.; Pieper, P.; and Zimmermann, E. *Die Darmstädter Pessach-Haggadah* (facsimile). Berlin, 1971–1972 (2 vols.).

———, ed. *The Dura-Europos Synagogue: A Re-Evaluation (1932–1972).* Missoula, Mont., 1973.

———. "Abraham in the Fire of the Chaldeans: A Jewish Legend in Jewish, Christian and Islamic Art," *Frühmittelalterliche Studien* 7 (1973): 342–352.

———, ed. *The Temple of Solomon: Archaeological Fact and Mediaeval Tradition in Christian, Islamic and Jewish Art.* Missoula, Mont., 1976.

———, ed. *The Image and the Word: Confrontations in Judaism, Christianity and Islam.* Missoula, Mont., 1977.

Hillgarth, J. N. and Narkiss, B. "A List of Hebrew Books (1330) and a Contract to Illuminate Manuscripts (1335) from Majorca," *Revue des études juives* 120 (1961): 297–320.

Italiener, B.; Freimann, A.; Mayer, A. L.; and Schmidt, A. *Die Darmstädter Pessach-Haggadah* (facsimile). Leipzig, 1927–1928 (2 vols.).

Katz, E. and Narkiss, B. *Machsor Lipsiae* (facsimile). Leipzig, 1964 (2 vols.).

Landsberger, F. "The Cincinnati Haggadah and its Decorator," *Hebrew Union College Annual* 15 (1940): 529–558.

Leveen, J. *The Hebrew Bible in Art.* New York, 1974².

Mayer, A. L. *Bibliography of Jewish Art.* Jerusalem, 1967.

Metzger, M. "Les illustrations bibliques d'un manuscrit hébreu du Nord de la France (1278–1340 environ)," *Mélanges offerts à René Crozet.* Poitiers, 1966: 1237–1253.

———. *La Haggada enluminée. Étude iconographique et stylistique des manuscrits enluminés et décorés de la Haggada du XIIIe au XVIe siècle,* I. Leiden, 1973.

———. "Un mahzor italien enluminé du XVe siècle," *Mitteilungen des Kunsthistorischen Institutes in Florenz* 20 (1976): 159–196.

Metzger, T. "Les objets du culte, le Sanctuaire du desert et le Temple de Jérusalem, dans les bibles hébraïques médiévales enluminées, en Orient et en Espagne," *Bulletin of the John Rylands Library* 52 (1970): 397–436; 53 (1970): 167–209.

———. "Le manuscrit enluminé Cod. Hebr. 5 de la Bibliothèque d'État à Munich," *Études de civilisation médiévale (IXe–XIIe siècles). Mélanges offerts à Edmond-René Labande.* Poitiers, 1974: 537–552.

———. *Les manuscrits hébreux copiés et décorés à Lisbonne dans les dernières décennies du XVe siècle.* Paris [Braga], 1977.

———. "Les illustrations d'un psautier hébreu italien de la fin du XIIIe siècle. Le Ms. Parm. 1870—de Rossi 510 de la Bibliothèque Palatine de Parma," *Cahiers archéologiques* 26 (1977): 145-162.

Monumenta Judaica. 2000 Jahre Geschichte und Kultur der Juden am

Rhein. Catalogue of Exhibition, Kölnisches Stadtmuseum. Cologne, 1964 (2 vols.).

Müller, D. H.; Schlosser, J. v.; and Kaufmann, D. *Die Haggadah von Sarajevo* (facsimile). Vienna, 1898 (2 vols.).

Narkiss, B. "A Tripartite Illuminated Mahzor from a South German School of Hebrew Illuminated Manuscripts around 1300," *Papers of the Fourth World Congress of Jewish Studies* II (1968): 125–133.

———. "An Illuminated *Mishneh Torah* in the Jewish National and University Library," *Kirjath Sepher* 43 (1968): 285–300 (in Hebrew).

———. *Hebrew Illuminated Manuscripts.* New York, 1969.

———. *The Golden Haggadah* (facsimile). London, 1970 (2 vols.).

——— and Sed-Rajna, G. *Index of Jewish Art. Iconographical Index of Hebrew Illuminated Manuscripts,* I. Jerusalem-Paris, 1976.

La paléographie hébraïque médiévale (Colloques internationaux du Centre National de la Recherche Scientifique, Paris, 1972, No. 547). Paris, 1974.

Panofsky, E. "Giotto and Maimonides in Avignon. The Story of an Illustrated Hebrew Manuscript," *The Journal of the Walters Art Gallery* 4 (1941): 27–44; 5 (1942): 124–127.

Roth, C. "Medieval Illustrations of Mouse Traps," *The Bodleian Library Record* 5 (1956): 244–252.

———. *The Kennicott Bible.* Oxford, 1957.

———. *The Aberdeen Codex of the Hebrew Bible.* Edinburgh, 1958.

———. *The Sarajevo Haggadah* (facsimile). New York, 1963.

Scheiber, A. *The Kaufmann Haggadah* (facsimile). Budapest, 1957.

Sed-Rajna, G. *Manuscrits hébreux de Lisbonne.* Paris, 1970.

———. "Toledo or Burgos?" *Journal of Jewish Art* 2 (1975): 6–21.

Sirat, C. and Beit-Arie, M. *Manuscrits médiévaux en caractères hébraïques portant des indications de date jusqu'à 1540,* I. Paris, 1972.

Sirat, C. *Écriture et civilisations.* Paris, 1976.

Spitzer, M.; Goldschmidt, E. D.; Jaffé, H. L. C.; Narkiss, B.; and Schapiro, M. *The Birds' Head Haggada* (facsimile). Jerusalem, 1967 (2 vols.).

Stassof, V. and Günzburg, D. *L'ornement hébreu.* Berlin, 1905.

Striedl, H. "Die Miniaturen in einer Handschrift des jüdisch-persischen Ardašīrbuches von Šāhīn," *Forschungsberichte* (Forschungen und Fortschritte der Katalogisierung der Orientalischen Handschriften in Deutschland, ed. W. Voigt) 10 (1966): 119–133.

Synagoga. Jüdische Altertümer, Handschriften und Kultgeräte. Catalogue of Exhibition at Historisches Museum. Frankfurt, 1961.

Wischnitzer, R. "Maimonides' Drawings of the Temple," *Journal of Jewish Art* 1 (1974): 16–27.

Wormald, F. "Afterthoughts on the Stockholm Exhibition," *Konsthistorisk Tidskrift* 22 (1953): 75–84.

LIST OF COLOR PLATES

I. **Pentateuch**
London, British Library,
Ms. Or. 2348
Sana'a, Yemen, 1469
415 X 280 mm

Plate 1. *Carpet Page,* fol. 38v
Plate 2. *Carpet Page,* fol. 155

II. **Ardašīr Book**
Tübingen, Universitätsbibliothek, Ms. Or. qu. 1680
Isfahan region, Persia, second half of seventeenth century
155 X 215 mm

Plate 3. *Bešōtan Gathers Maidens about Šāh Bahman,* fol. 29
Plate 4. *Mordecai Hanging the Sons of Haman,* fol. 93

III. **Bible**
Jerusalem, Jewish National and University Library, Ms. Heb. 4°790
Burgos, Spain, 1260
302 X 270 mm

Plate 5. *Carpet Page,* fol. 114

IV. **Bible**
Paris, Bibliothèque Nationale, Ms. hébr. 7
Perpignan, Aragon, 1299
320 X 237 mm

Plate 6. *Sanctuary Vessels,* fol. 12v
Plate 7. *Sanctuary Vessels,* fol. 13

V. **Bible**
Parma, Biblioteca Palatina, Ms. Parm. 2810 (de Rossi 518)
Spain, second quarter of fourteenth century
228 X 205 mm

Plate 8. *Sanctuary Vessels,* fol. 7v
Plate 9. *Sanctuary Vessels,* fol. 8

VI. **Bible**
Lisbon, Biblioteca Nacional de Lisboa,
Ms. Hebr. 72
Cervera, Spain, 1300
282 X 217 mm

Plate 10. *Artist's Colophon,* fol. 449

VII. **Golden Haggadah**
London, British Library,
Ms. Add. 27210
Catalonia, Spain, 1320–1330
247 X 195 mm

Plate 11. *Childhood of Moses,* fol. 9
Plate 12. *Plagues of Egypt,* fol. 12v

VIII. **Rylands Haggadah**
Manchester, The John Rylands University Library,
Library, Ms. 6
Valencia (?), Spain, second quarter of fourteenth century
280 X 230 mm

Plate 13. *Crossing the Red Sea,* fol. 19
Plate 14. *Celebration of Passover,* fol. 19v

IX. **Sarajevo Haggadah**
Sarajevo, Zemaljski Musej,
Catalonia, Spain, third quarter of fourteenth century (?)
220 X 160 mm

Plate 15. *Israelites in the Desert,* fol. 29
Plate 16. *Revelation at Sinai,* fol. 30

X. **Commentary to the Bible**
Munich, Bayrische Staatsbibliothek, Ms. Hebr. 5/II
Würzburg area, Germany, 1233
380 X 285 mm

Plate 17. *Three Hebrews in the Fiery Furnace,* II, fol. 209

XI. **Schocken Bible**
Jerusalem, Schocken Institute Library,
Ms. 14840
Southwest Germany, early fourteenth century
220 X 150 mm

Plate 18. *Frontispiece to Genesis,* fol. 1v

XII. **Pentateuch**
London, British Library,
Ms. Add. 15282
Southern Germany, early fourteenth century
228 X 162 mm

Plate 19. *Frontispiece to Deuteronomy,* fol. 238

XIII. **Miscellany**
London, British Library,
Ms. Add. 11639
Northeast France, last quarter of thirteenth century
157 X 122 mm

Plate 20. *David Playing the Harp,* fol. 117v
Plate 21. *David and Goliath,* fol. 523v

XIV. Pentateuch
Copenhagen, The Royal Library, Ms. Hebr. 11
Bavaria, Germany, early fourteenth century
395 X 295 mm

Plate 22. *Micrographic Frontispiece to Leviticus,* fol. 104v

XV. Mishneh Torah of Maimonides
Budapest, Library of the Hungarian Academy of Sciences, Kaufmann Collection, Ms. A 77/I
Germany, 1295–1296
500 X 350 mm

Plate 23. *Frontispiece, Book II,* fol. 46v

XVI. Leipzig Mahzor
Leipzig, Karl-Marx-Universitätsbibliothek, Ms. V. 1102/I–II
Upper Rhine, Germany, first quarter of fourteenth century
I, 496 X 363 mm;
II, 485 X 385 mm

Plate 24. *Hanging of Haman and his Sons (Purim),* I, fol. 51v
Plate 25. *Abraham in the Fire (Yom Kippur),* II, fol. 164v
Plate 26. *Leviathan and Behemoth (Sukkot),* II, fol. 181v

XVII. Mahzor
London, British Library, Ms. Add. 22413
Southern Germany, first quarter of fourteenth century
315 X 220 mm

Plate 27. *Revelation at Sinai (Shavuot),* fol. 3
Plate 28. *Ruth and Boaz (Shavuot),* fol. 71

XVIII. Darmstadt Haggadah
Darmstadt: Hessische Landes- und Hochschulbibliothek, Ms. Or. 8
Upper Rhine, Germany, ca. 1430
355 X 245 mm

Plate 29. *Decorative Page,* fol. 48v

XIX. Miscellany
Hamburg, Staats-und Universitätsbibliothek, Ms. Hebr. 37
Middle Rhine, Germany, second quarter of fifteenth century
300 X 220 mm

Plate 30. *The Messiah at the Passover Seder,* fol. 35v
Plate 31. *Scenes of Martyrdom (Hanukkah),* fol. 79

XX. Haggadah
London, British Library, Ms. Add. 14762
Northern Italy (?) and Germany, 1460–1470
375 X 280 mm

Plate 32. *Five Rabbis of Benei Berak,* fol. 7v

XXI. Arba'a Turim of Jacob ben Asher
Rome, Biblioteca Apostolica Vaticana, Ms. Ross. 555
Mantua, Italy, 1435
335 X 235 mm

Plate 33. *Slaughtering of Animals,* between fols. 127–128
Plate 34. *Wedding,* fol. 220

XXII. Canon of Medicine of Avicenna
Bologna, Biblioteca Universitaria di Bologna, Ms. 2197
North Italy, third quarter of fifteenth century (?)
430 X 290 mm

Plate 35. *Urinoscopy,* fol. 23v

XXIII. Sefer ha-Ikkarim of Joseph Albo
Rovigo, Biblioteca dell Accademia dei Concordi, Ms. Silvestriana 220
Florence, 1460–1470
360 X 250 mm

Plate 36. *Frontispiece,* Book I, fol. 9

XXIV. Rothschild Miscellany
Jerusalem, Israel Museum, Ms. 180/51
North Italy, third quarter of fifteenth century
210 X 160 mm

Plate 37. *Job,* fol. 64v
Plate 38. *Rosh ha-Shanah Page,* fol. 132v

XXV. Bible
Paris, Bibliothèque Nationale, Ms. hébr. 15
Lisbon, Portugal, end of fifteenth century and central Italy, early sixteenth century
320 X 247 mm

Plate 39. *Frontispiece to Joshua,* fol. 137v
Plate 40. *Frontispiece to Chronicles,* fol. 374v

LIST OF BLACK-AND-WHITE FIGURES

PLATES AND COMMENTARIES

Since Hebrew manuscripts read from right to left, rather than left to right as in Western (Christian) manuscripts, those pages which are "recto" folios are left-hand pages in Hebrew manuscripts, and "verso" folios are right-hand pages. (An exception occurs in the *Sarajevo Haggadah,* where the miniatures were painted on only the fleshy side of the vellum, so that the folios are numbered without any verso indications.) This reading from right to left will explain the placement of Plates 7–6, 9–8, and 16–15, which face each other here as they do in the original manuscripts.

PLATE 1

PENTATEUCH

fol. 38v *Carpet Page*

Dating from 1469 in Sana'a, Yemen, this Pentateuch page typifies a group of miniatures made in fifteenth-century Yemen. Dominated by a large outer circle, this folio also has a smaller inner roundel within which is a six-pointed star design, its triangular spaces filled with arabesques. Between the two circles are five paired fish—three arranged head to tail, one pair intertwined back to back, and the fifth pair head to head. The central disc is held by two roughly triangular shapes which overlap the circumference of the outer circular design. They have scale patterns that give the appearance of a mountain. The space surrounding the circular design and the frame is filled with arabesques. Placed on the paper of the manuscript, these patterns in rose, violet, dark green, and blue serve as a chromatic background. The colors are the same as those employed in Islamic enameled glass objects of the period. The lower edge of the page has a rope pattern. All designs—the scales, fish, roundels, and star—are composed of micrographic verses taken from Psalms 119 and 121 and seem to have no bearing on the depictions.

The design of the large roundel—the star pattern and fish—is closely related to interior bottoms of metal bowls and basins found in Egypt, Syria, and Persia from the thirteenth century onward, and these designs may have been the source of inspiration. The slightly curved triangular shapes with scale patterns, which may symbolize mountains, have artistic antecedents in ancient Near and Far Eastern art, but the Hebrew micrography itself is apparently unparalleled in Islamic decorations.

The whole composition may represent a Muslim cosmological design. The sun may be in the center; a circular body of water—the ocean—with fish may surround the earth, which is held together by the mountain Qāf. This symbolic picture may also be readable in biblical terms as Psalm 104:5–6 has it:

> He established the earth upon its foundations that it
> shall never totter. *Tehom* (ocean) covered it like a garment.
> The waters stood against the mountains.

1

PLATE 2

PENTATEUCH

fol. 155 *Carpet Page*

Entirely different is the splendid carpet page at the end of the manuscript. Arabesque borders frame the entire page. The design in the center resembles a dome on pendentives. Within the roundel is an intersecting square with intertwining arabesques traceable to earlier mosaic patterns. The quatrefoil design around the circle, reminiscent of the arches supporting the dome, is filled with arabesque designs as are the surrounding spandrels. The inscription in Arabic in this folio and folio 154v reads: "This manuscript was finished in the month of Safar of the year 874 (1469 A.D.) Property of Ibrahīm ibn Yūsuf ibn Sā'īd (ibn) Ibrahīm al-Isrā'īlī." The page, not only in decoration, but in text, is outspokenly Arabic, even to the use of the Muslim month and year and the Arabic equivalent for the Hebrew names Abraham and Joseph. It is quite likely that the scribe, who did not sign his name to this manuscript, but was responsible for several related manuscripts, was Banyah ben Saadiah ben Zechariah ben Margaz.

The decorated pages, which may also be from this artist's hand, constitute definite evidence of Jewish artistic activity in Yemen, differing in this respect from unsigned, surviving Yemenite metal objects, all probably made by Jews, since they exclusively controlled this craft, which was considered unworthy and inferior by Muslims. Most of the decorative motifs belong to the stock in trade of Islamic art. Unfortunately, we have little evidence available concerning contemporary Muslim Yemenite manuscripts and thus are unable to compare them with the Hebrew manuscripts.

The gold and lapis lazuli colors favored by Mamluk court artists have been replaced here by the simpler pigments of red, green, and blue, in keeping with a provincial center. The artist who decorated this manuscript has skillfully combined artistic features derived from both the Jewish and Islamic traditions.

29
גמע אורדן בשותן דוכתראן אז
אטראף שאה בזמין
צראחה סכן צו דר מעאט
אז עקד בגשוד גוהר נאב
בגשוד דר גוהר
כה גוהר קימתי בהר באב

3

PLATE 3

Ardašīr Book

fol. 29 *Bešōtan gathers maidens about Šāh Bahman*

This typical Safavid miniature comes from an illuminated epos known as the *Ardašīr Book,* composed in Judeo-Persian (Hebrew letters and Persian language) in 1332 by Maulānā Šāhīn, a Jewish poet. It is part of a larger work, an epos of the Bible—the Jewish past—shaped after Firdausi's classical tenth-century *Šāh-nāmeh*—an epos of the Iranian past.

The *Ardašīr Book* may have been illuminated in the fourteenth century, but only two illuminated copies are extant (this manuscript and New York: Library of the Jewish Theological Seminary of America, Acc. No. 40919). The introductory chapter of the *Ardašīr Book* is taken from Firdausi's *Šāh-nāmeh,* to which is skillfully appended the biblical story of Esther with embellishments from Jewish and Muslim legends and from Šāhīn's creative imagination. The Book of Esther, with its Persian setting, lent itself beautifully to Šāhīn's talents. The heroes of the Book are Ardašīr (or Bahman), who is identified with the biblical Ahasuerus, and his sons Šērō and Kūroš (Cyrus). Especially interesting are those miniatures dealing with the story of Esther. Esther illustrations are, of course, familiar in medieval Jewish and Christian art and became popular in the cycle of Esther scrolls illustrated in Europe from the seventeenth century onward. Such illustrations are, however, not found in Islamic art.

The first miniature related to the Esther story is based on the biblical account (Esther 2:8—9) and depicts King Ahasuerus seeking a new queen after having deposed Vashti. The caption to this miniature reads: "Bešōtan gathers the daughters of the surrounding areas about Šāh Bahman." In the center sits the king on his intarsia throne pedestal, wearing a crown bedecked with jewels and a feather. A servant at his side offers him wine. The same servant, also holding the wine container, may be one of the seven chosen maidens cited in the text. Six gesturing maidens—one plays a tambourine—are arranged in a semicircle around Ardašīr. They are seated on a light orange rug with floral ornamentation. The tapestry covering the wall has a bird and rabbit pattern, typical of contemporary Persian miniatures. The crown, headdresses, garments, and stylistic characteristics of this miniature bear striking similarities to a *Khamsa* of Nizāmī miniature, dated Isfahan, 1650 (Paris: Bibl. Nat., supp. pers. 1111, fol. 184v), probably made by the painter Tālib. Our miniature is, without doubt, a provincial rendering of the court art of Isfahan.

בר דאר זדן מרדכי דה פוסראן
המן לעין רא

PLATE 4

Ardašīr Book

fol. 93 *Mordecai hanging the sons of Haman*

"Mordecai hanging the ten sons of the accursed Haman," reads the inscription to this miniature, based, of course, upon the biblical account (Esther 9:7–10, 13–14); the ten sons are shown hanging from the gallows. Unable to fit all the sons into the format used for the other miniatures, the artist simply widened his picture plane and shortened its height accordingly. Each of the ten sons is suspended from a red rope on the gallows. Most are shown in profile, some in three-quarter view, one in full view, and the one in the center is depicted from behind, although his feet are unnaturally turned outward. Apparently the artist was not successful in the foreshortening of the feet. Most of the figures are shown barefoot, still wearing their bright garments—orange, purple, olive-green, gold-yellow; the far left figure has been stripped of his outer garment and wears pants only.

At the bottom are four archers on horseback, three of them turbaned and turning outward, one figure wearing a crown—perhaps to indicate Mordecai—turning inward. The figures appear more animated and realistic in their facial expressions and different body postures than the rather schematic and puppetlike rendering of figures in the other miniatures. The mounted archers, placed directly below, rather than in front of, the hanging figures, appear to be shooting beyond their target. In typical Persian ladder perspective, little difference is made between fore and background or in the size of the figures.

Small tufts of grass, the scalloped edges of the mountaintop, and a strip of blue above the gallows are the subtle indications of a landscape setting. The vivid colors, the small horses, the shooting of arrows at men suspended from gallows are encountered in *Šāh-nāmeh* and other Persian Safavid miniatures which the artist undoubtedly used as a model. The hanging of Haman and his sons is often illustrated in Jewish art in the lands of Western Christendom from the thirteenth century onward (Plate 24), but in a manner that bears no iconographic relation to this depiction. In *mahzorim* of Western Europe, Haman and his sons are usually suspended from the branches of a tree.

5

PLATE 5

BIBLE

fol. 114 *Carpet Page*

The miniature comes from a Spanish manuscript written by Menahem ben Abraham Malik in Burgos in 1260. It is among the earliest Hebrew illuminations from Spain that have survived. Burgos, along with Toledo, produced Bible manuscripts renowned for the accuracy of their texts and the excellent quality of their script. As in most manuscripts from these centers, ornamental carpet pages usually proceed or follow the main divisions of the Hebrew Bible—a practice that probably originated in Islamic Hebrew Bibles and was shared with illuminated *Qur'ān* manuscripts. This miniature is placed before the Prophets, the second of the three divisions of the Hebrew Bible. A typical carpet page, it is framed by one line of *masorah* written in bold *Sephardi* script between two lines of micrographic *masorah*. Springing from a central stem on either side are elegant scrolls, with interlacings and fillets that bear palmette and floral designs. These forms are filled with gold and flanked on both sides by lines of micrography, which are placed on the uncolored parchment ground. The spaces in between the designs have a light-colored wash background of purple, green, and brown.

Few examples from Burgos have survived, but the ornamented carpet pages reveal a close kinship to carpet pages from Toledo, especially those manuscripts written by the scribe Isaac ben Israel. The basic pattern of these pages can be traced to Islamic wall decorations. Similar designs can be found in the wooden panels from the eighth-century Aqsa mosque in Jerusalem. With the establishment of the Umayyad caliphate in Spain, these decorations traveled westward and can be seen in the tenth-century mosque of Cordoba. From Toledo itself, a carved marble panel from the end of the eleventh century shows similar scrolls, with palmette and pine cones, done in a more naturalistic vein than in this miniature (Archaeological Museum, Province of Toledo).

PLATE 7

BIBLE

fol. 13 *Sanctuary Vessels*

Arranged in three compartments, we behold the golden incense altar (*mizbah ha-ketoret,* Exodus 30:1), with the two silver trumpets (*hatzotzrot,* Numbers 10:2) and the horn (*shofar,* Leviticus 25:9) underneath it. In the left compartment is the altar of burnt offering (*mizbah ha-olah,* Exodus 27:1ff.), its copper grating of mesh work (*ma'ase reshet,* Exodus 27:4), and the laver *(kiyyor)* with its stand (*kan,* Exodus 30:18). At the bottom are the pots *(sirot)* for the ashes, the basins *(mizrakot)* for the blood of the sacrifices, the triangular shovels or scrapers *(ya'im)* for the removal of ashes, the flesh hooks *(mizlagot)* for turning the broiling meat, and the firepans *(mahtot)* to carry the hot coals (Exodus 27:3). The explanation for the insertion of these cultic images in the opening pages of the Spanish Hebrew Bibles is to be found in the inscription surrounding the blue frame: "All [implements existed] while the Temple was upon its site and the holy Sanctuary was upon its foundation. Blessed is he who beheld it in all its glory and splendor and [witnessed] all the acts of its power and might. And happy he who waits and comes to see it. May it be Your will that it [the Temple] be speedily rebuilt in our days so that our eyes may behold it and our heart rejoice."

To strengthen and insure this fervent desire to behold the Temple in the messianic future, the Spanish Jew not only prayed daily for its restoration, but placed in his Bibles a visual image of the Sanctuary vessels which, according to rabbinic tradition, had been hidden by King Josiah or God himself, but would be returned in messianic times. Placement of the Sanctuary vessels of the future Solomonic Temple in Bible manuscripts has no apparent antecedents in Christian or Jewish art. The Byzantine Octateuchs and the *Codex Amiatinus* feature only the vessels of the wilderness Tabernacle, and these cultic utensils offer hardly any convincing parallels to the depictions in the Spanish Hebrew Bibles.

A miniature from a manuscript of the *Book of Knowledge of Ingenious Mechanical Devices* by al-Jazarī, made around 1315 in northern Mesopotamia, shows an automaton of a kneeling female slave holding a water pitcher with a dragon spout that resembles the laver with dragon spouts in this miniature, indicating that some of the models for the holy cultic implements probably were Islamic ceramic and metal vessels.

PLATE 6

Bible

fol. 12v *Sanctuary Vessels*

Written and possibly illuminated by Solomon ben Raphael in 1299 at Perpignan, Aragon, this manuscript is probably the earliest example of a unique iconographic tradition originating in late thirteenth-century Spain.

It became customary to adorn the preliminary folios of Hebrew Bibles with the cult objects that, according to rabbinic tradition, had once graced the ancient Solomonic Temple. Surrounding the blue frame is an inscription in red *Sephardi* lettering: "Now this is how the lampstand was made: it was hammered work of gold, hammered from base to petals. According to the pattern that the Lord had shown Moses, so was the lampstand made (Numbers 8:4). And on the lampstand itself there shall be four cups shaped like almond blossoms, each with calyx and petals (Exodus 25:34)." In keeping with the inscription we see the golden lampstand *(menorah),* its tongs *(malkahayim),* and snuffers (*mahtot,* Exodus 25:38), the jar of *manna* (*tzintzenet ha-man,* Exodus 16:33) flanked by the barren rod *(mateh)* and the budding rod of Aaron (Numbers 17:18), the cherubim *(keruvim)* seated on the ark cover (*kapporet,* Exodus 25:17ff.), the table of showbread (*shulhan ha-tahor,* Exodus 25:23ff.), and the tablets of the Ten Commandments. It should be noted that the opening Hebrew words of each of the Ten Commandments are given (Exodus 20 and Deuteronomy 5). As the opening word of the Fourth Commandment varies in the two versions, *zakhor* (*remember* the Sabbath, Exodus 20:8) and *shamor* (*observe* the Sabbath, Deuteronomy 5:12), both are inserted. The two pans of frankincense above the table of showbread, the arrangement of the loaves of showbread in compartments on the table, the cherubim with the faces of bearded youths, the blue stone *(even)* with three steps flanking the lampstand, the decorative elements of the lampstand with its six flames turning to the central flame are not mentioned in the Bible, but closely follow the description of these objects found in the eighth book (*Avodah,* the *Book of Temple Service*) of the *Mishneh Torah*, the legal code of the twelfth-century Spanish Jewish philosopher Maimonides.

כל אלה כהיות היכל על מכונתו ומקדש הקדש

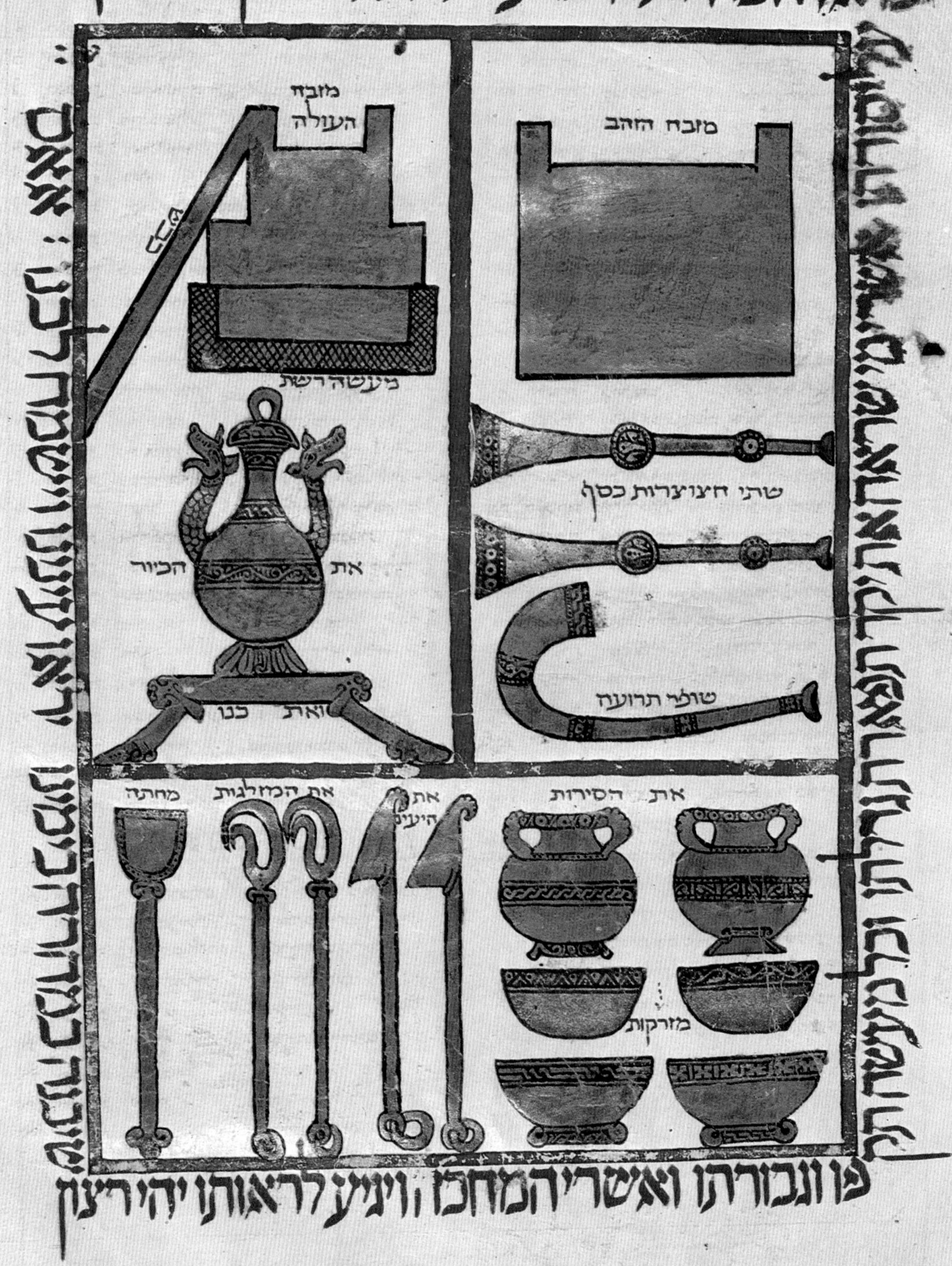

פו וגבורתו ואשרי המחכה ויגיע לראותו יהי רצון

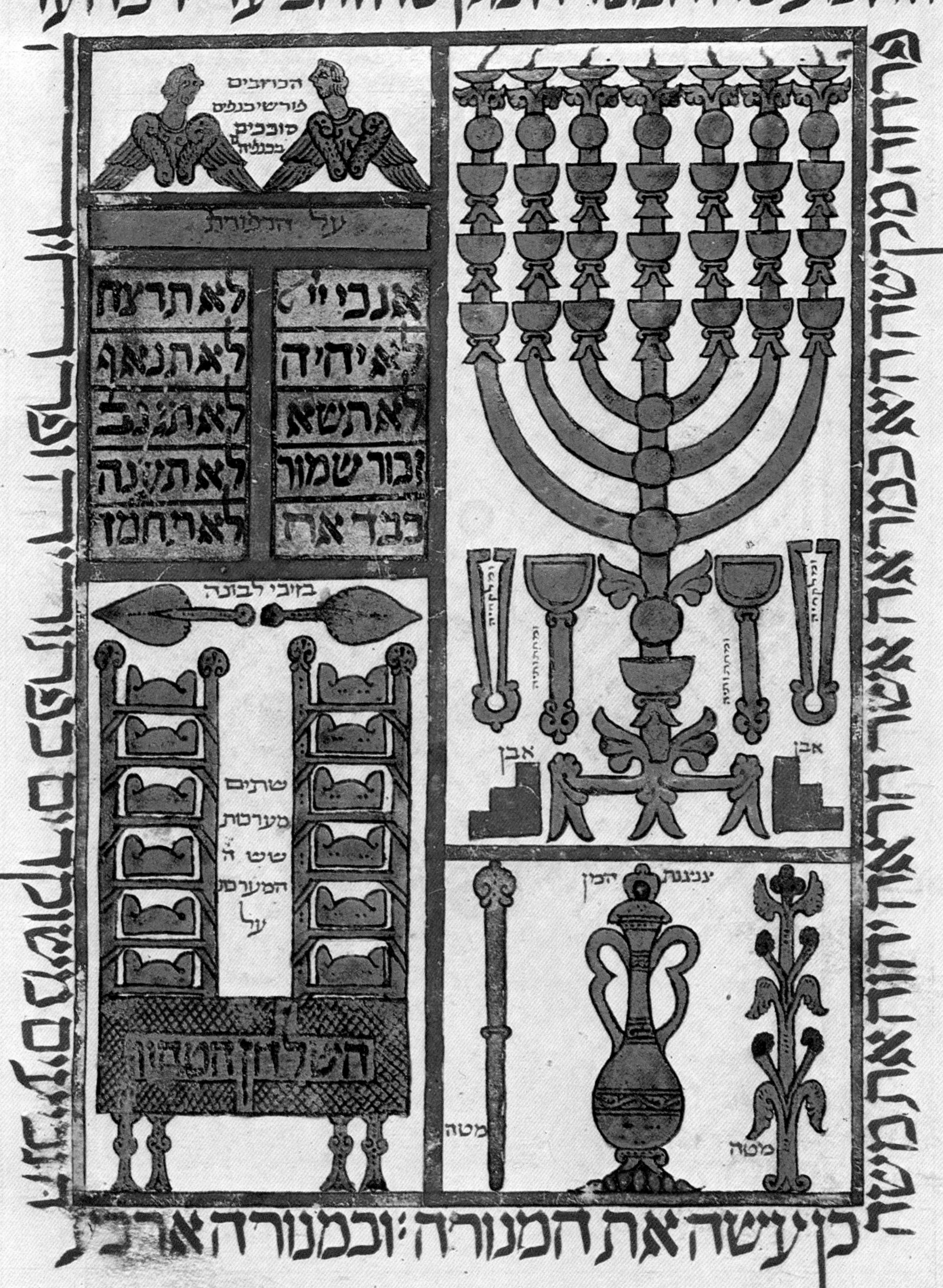

וזה מעשה המנרה מקשה זהב עד ירכה עד
הכרובים פורשי כנפים סוככים בכנפיהם
על הכפורת
אנכי ה׳
לא יהיה
לא תשא
זכור שמור
כבד את
לא תרצח
לא תנאף
לא תגנב
לא תענה
לא תחמד
בזיכי לבונה
שתים מערכות שש המערכת על
השלחן
אבן
אבן
צנצנת המן
מטה
מטה
כן עשה את המנורה: וכמנורה

PLATE 9

BIBLE

fol. 8 *Sanctuary Vessels*

The implements are once again set against the alternating red-green-blue diapered fields. We note that the cherubim seated on the ark cover have been eliminated. The tablets of the Ten Commandments are divided horizontally; the words are barely legible against the black stippled background. The ark is, moreover, outfitted with the prescribed four rings and the two poles (*taba'ot* and *badim,* Exodus 25:12). The barren rod, the incense pans, an altar, and some of the pots and basins of the earlier miniature are missing. The laver looks like a long-stemmed chalice rather than the dragon-spouted pitcher.

Perhaps the most important innovation of this and other miniatures is the depiction of a small mound which has a stylized tree atop it. In two fourteenth-century Spanish Hebrew miniatures, this mound is identified as the Mount of Olives (*har ha-zeitim*). What is the meaning of the Mount of Olives amidst the Sanctuary vessels? One manuscript, dated 1404, from Saragossa (Paris: Bibl. Nat., Ms. hébr. 31, fol. 4) has a page devoted to the Mount of Olives. Around the illustration of the mount runs an inscription from Zechariah 14:4: "And his feet shall stand on that day on the Mount of Olives which lies before Jerusalem on the east; and the Mount of Olives shall be split in two from east to west by a very wide valley." A mural in the third-century synagogue of Dura-Europos illustrates this momentous event. A cleft Mount of Olives, topped by two olive trees, discharges on Resurrection Day the corpses of the righteous buried within. The meaning of the Mount of Olives is clear. The righteous dead, on that final day, will, according to rabbinic tradition, emerge from the Mount of Olives in Jerusalem and be enabled to view, from that vantage point, the beautiful cultic vessels of the Third Temple—the rebuilt Messianic Temple.

PLATE 8

BIBLE

fol. 7v *Sanctuary Vessels*

The iconographic tradition established in 1299 by the Aragonese miniatures, or their models, continued in several Bible manuscripts until the early fourteenth century. By the second quarter of the fourteenth century, the introduction of distinct iconographic and stylistic variations is noticeable. Several of these manuscripts are closely related (London: British Library, Ms. Add. 15250 and Ms. Harl. 1528; and a Pentateuch in Istanbul's Hasköy Karaite Synagogue is actually dated 1336). Alternating diapered compartments of green, red, and blue are employed as background—typical of Gothic miniatures—against which is placed the golden lampstand that occupies the whole page. The stone used by the priest to trim the lampstand has six steps, and the implements for servicing the *menorah* are here suspended from its branches. The inscriptions around the borders of the miniature have been eliminated.

According to the Bible, the seven-branched golden lampstand was fashioned by Bezalel for the wilderness Tabernacle. It was not found in the original Solomonic Temple, but stood in the Second Temple (as it is depicted on the Arch of Titus in Rome as one of the spoils taken from Jerusalem by the Romans in 70 A.D.). It became a symbol of Judaism and is featured in many catacombs and synagogues excavated and dating back to between the third and sixth centuries A.D. In the Middle Ages, the seven-branched lampstand could be found in many Christian churches as a type or prefiguration of Christ. In the Spanish Hebrew Bibles, it is prominently displayed as one of the vessels of the rebuilt and hoped-for Third Jerusalem Temple.

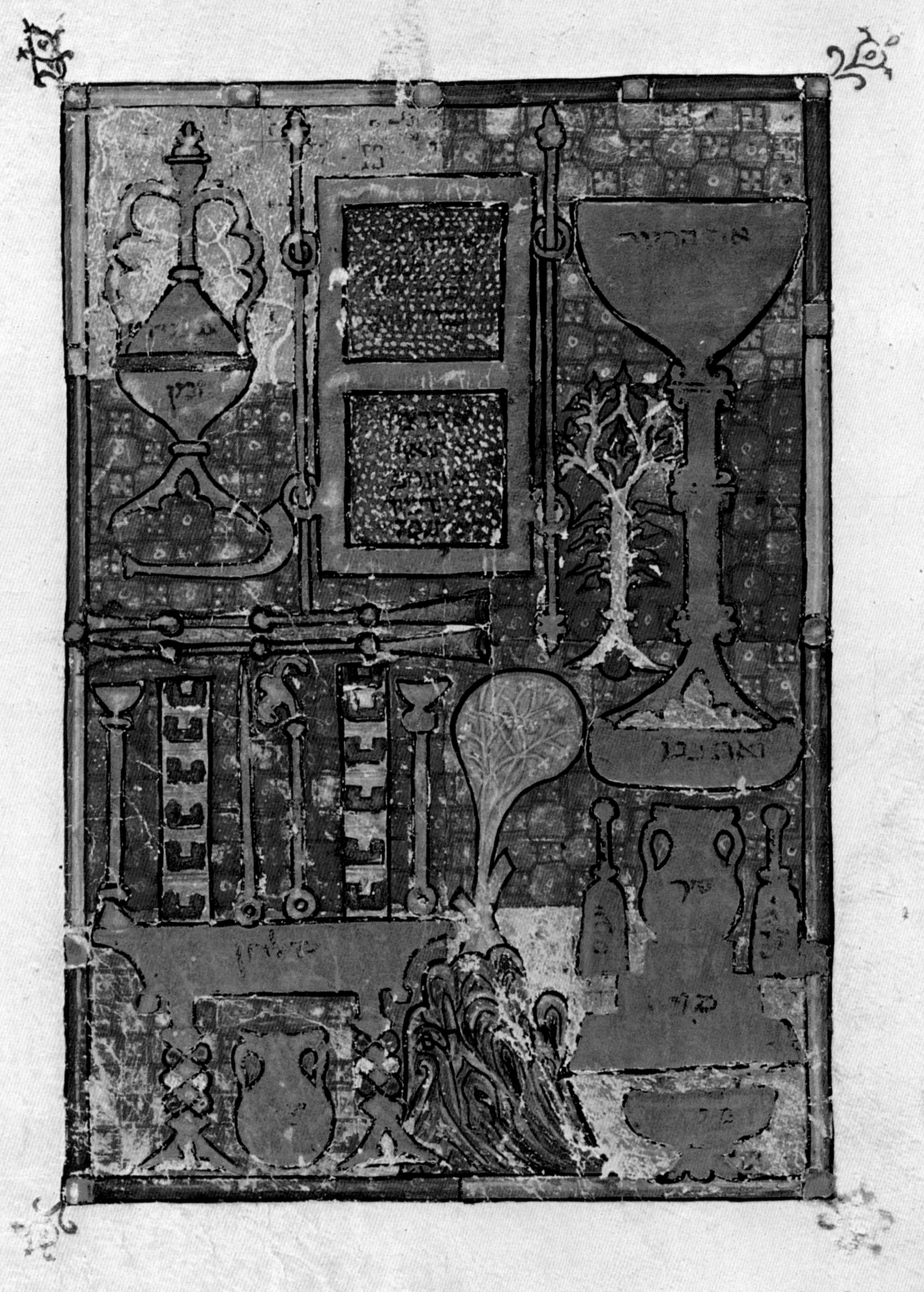

9

PLATE 10

Bible

fol. 449 *Artist's Colophon*

This zoomorphic and anthropomorphic page has the signature of the artist: "I, Joseph the Frenchman, illustrated and completed this book." It is one of the few Hebrew manuscripts signed by a Jewish artist. The scribe of the Bible, Samuel ben Abraham ibn Nathan, finished it at Cervera between 1299–1300.

Differing from most other Spanish Hebrew Bible manuscripts of the period, this one has text illustrations. The signature is placed within a red frame divided by five panels, and the Hebrew letters have the rounded and elegant appearance so typical of *Sephardi* script. The *lamed* ascender and the *peh* descender break the outline of the panels. The letters themselves are made up of floral motifs, human heads, fish, birds, dogs, and other animal heads and bodies. The bird trying to hold a fish in its beak is an especially common motif in Latin letters found in Mozarabic manuscripts from the ninth to the eleventh centuries. It is at home, as well, in eighth to ninth-century Merovingian and Carolingian art. The use of zoomorphic and anthropomorphic letters is also known, from the twelfth century on, in Armenian manuscripts and in Islamic art. Several other Hebrew manuscripts from Spain and Germany [such as Berlin: Preussische Staatsbibliothek, Ms. Ham. 288 and Parma: Bibl. Palatina, Ms. Parm. 2422 (de Rossi 1107)] employ zoomorphic and anthropomorphic lettering. Whether this Bible was actually illuminated in the small Jewish community of Cervera or in a nearby larger Jewish community deserves study.

Most remarkable is the fact that this manuscript came to La Coruña in Spanish Galicia, where Joseph ibn Hayyim, the artist of the well-known late fifteenth-century *Kennicott Bible* (Oxford: Bodleian Library, Kennicott 1), used it as a model. The artist creatively adapted the signature of Joseph the Frenchman. No direct copy, his letters are more stylized, and he introduces different combinations of animals and nude human figures into his letters (Figure IX). Although differing in style, some other iconographic motifs in the *Kennicott Bible* clearly show the *Cervera Bible* as its source of inspiration. Some of these analogies are the text illustration of Jonah being thrown into the sea and swallowed by a huge fish, and the border motif of a mother hen feeding her chicks.

ותתצב אחותו
ונערותיה הולכות
בתיה מביאה משה לפני פר׳ה
איש מצרי מכה איש עברי
ויך את המצרי ויטמנהו בחול

11

PLATE 11

Golden Haggadah

fol. 9 *Childhood of Moses*

This miniature comes from one of the earliest surviving Spanish *Haggadot*—it precedes the liturgical text proper. Divided into four framed panels, each scene therein is set against a gold, diapered and studded, tooled background. The colored frame is decorated with delicate *rinceaux* and with golden squares. Slender tendrils with leaves are attached to the four corners of the entire folio.

Reading from right to left, we see the *Finding of the Child Moses in the Nile.* Miriam is seated on a hillock in keeping with the inscription: "And his sister stationed herself" (Exodus 2:4). Below her in the water three nude maidens are approaching, and the Hebrew inscription reads: "While her maidens walked" (Exodus 2:5). The girl in front is opening the lid of the casket in which lies the baby Moses wrapped in swaddling clothes. Deviating from the biblical text, the artist shows us the princess with her two maidens in the Nile waters. God, according to rabbinic legend, had scourged Pharaoh's daughter with sores and inflammation of the flesh. She sought relief from the burning pain in the Nile. Upon touching the casket containing Moses, she was miraculously healed of her affliction. The next episode depicts the enthroned Pharaoh, surrounded by three counsellors. Pharaoh's daughter, holding the infant Moses, is escorted by her two maidservants. The inscription: "Bithiah brings Moses before Pharaoh," is again taken from rabbinic literature; the Bible neither identifies Pharaoh's daughter nor relates this episode. Bottom right follows the inscription: "An Egyptian beating a Hebrew" (Exodus 2:11), and "He struck down the Egyptian and hid him in the sand" (Exodus 2:12). To the left of the tree, a kneeling Moses, holding an ax dripping with blood, is about to bury the slain Egyptian lying at his feet. In the last scene Moses is centered between two trees. In keeping with the inscription: "Moses rose to their defense" (Exodus 2:17), we see him admonishing two shepherds who intended to drive Jethro's sheep from the well. Three women stand behind him.

The miniatures of this *Haggadah* were probably painted in a Catalonian workshop between 1320 and 1330. Two artists worked on the miniatures. The hand of the first artist is discernible here—revealing a somewhat crude rendition of the elegant Gothic figures we associate with the High Gothic emanating from the schools of Paris.

PLATE 12

Golden Haggadah

fol. 12v *Plagues of Egypt*

The second artist who painted this miniature reveals greater mastery of the High Gothic idiom—in the beautiful S curves of the bodies, in the folds of the draperies, in the wavy, puffy hair, and the gestures of his figures.

An enthroned Pharaoh is placed before the multistoried, stylized palace architecture of the period. Moses (not Aaron, as the Bible has it) is touching the Nile with his rod, while green frogs leap out into vessels and towards Pharaoh. The inscription reads: "And the frogs came up" (Exodus 8:2). The next scene has Aaron, holding a staff, and Moses standing before Pharaoh and his wise men who are all covered with lice. Three women are peering from palace windows and on the ground such animals as oxen and donkeys are shown suffering from the plague of lice. The inscription reads: "And the vermin came upon man and beast" (Exodus 8:13). Below, Moses holds a rod. Wild beasts—a wolf, a lion, a dog—are attacking an astonished Pharaoh, who stands in front of what appears to be a baldachin. The inscription reads: "swarms of insects" (Exodus 8:20). The Hebrew word *arov,* according to rabbinic traditions, is rendered as "wild beasts." Christian illustrations, such as those of the twelfth- and thirteenth-century *Pamplona Bibles,* also follow this rabbinic interpretation. "Severe pestilence" (Exodus 9:3) is the inscription to the last scene. From the top of a fortified tower, two men are lowering a dead sheep and a goat. On the ground, dead donkeys, horses, and sheep are piled up. On either side of the tower are two mourning figures—one wiping away a tear and the other, in keeping with the inscription, "rending his garment."

The iconography of both artists reveals that they utilized mid-thirteenth-century manuscripts, such as the famous *Morgan Picture Bible* (New York: Morgan Library, Ms. 638) and the *Psalter of St. Louis* (Paris: Bibl. Nat., Ms. lat. 10525). In style, these miniatures are most closely related to a series of miniatures found in a manuscript of Catalan Laws (Paris: Bibl. Nat., Ms. lat. 4670A), made in Catalonia, perhaps in Barcelona, between 1320–1335. The handling of faces, hair, garments, and headgear shows the distinct French influence with some Italianate architectural features, especially in the spatial settings.

משה
ותעל הצפרדע
אהרן
משה
ותהי הכנם באדם ובבהמה

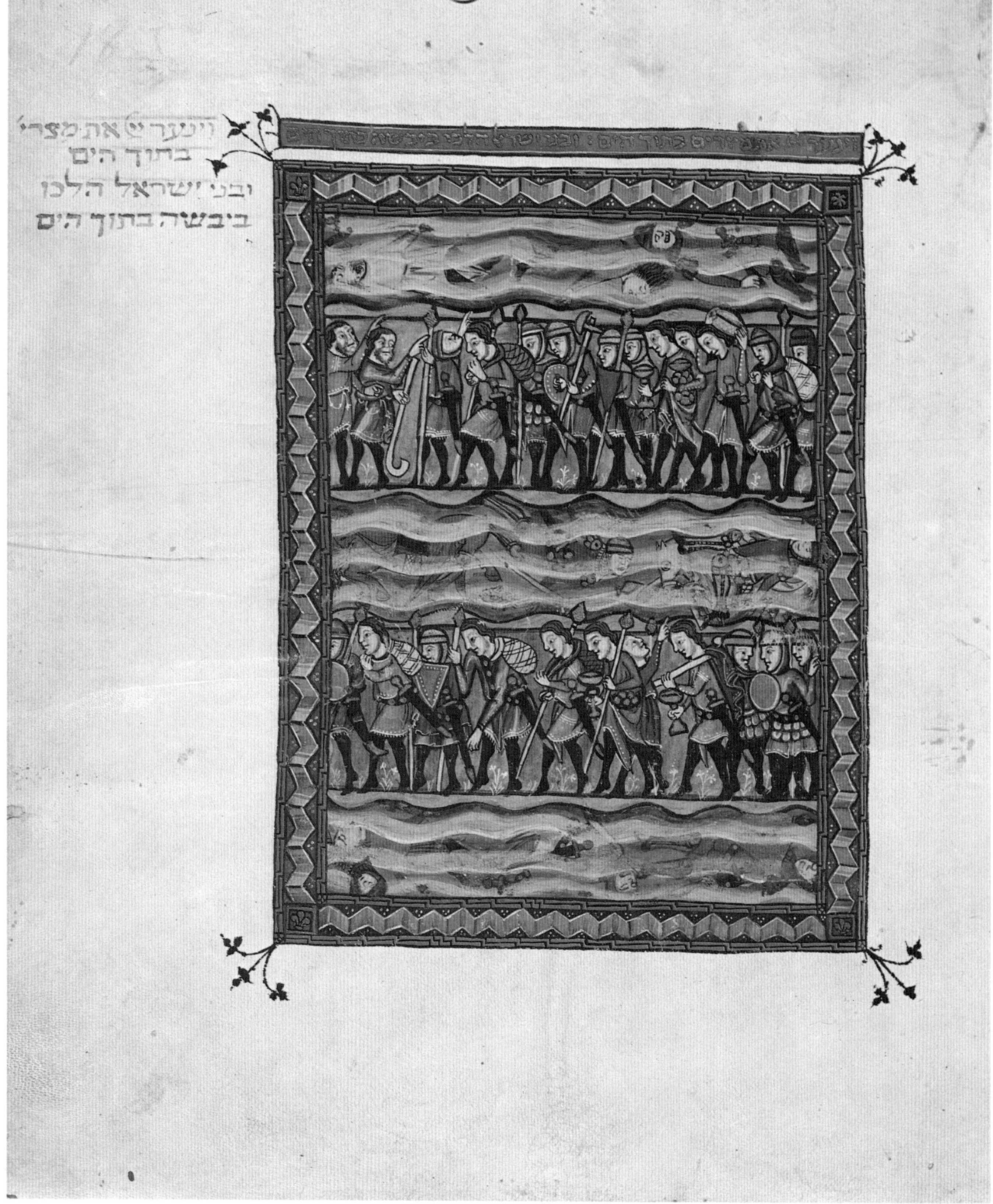
ויער ײ את מצרי'
בתוך הים
ובני ישראל הלכו
ביבשה בתוך הים

PLATE 13

Rylands Haggadah

fol. 19 *Crossing the Red Sea*

This *Haggadah* has a series of full-page miniatures preceding the liturgical text, as well as text illustrations. The *hors texte* miniatures of the first nineteen folios are mainly restricted to the Book of Exodus and contain few legendary amplifications of the biblical text.

The *Crossing of the Red Sea* has a narrow, oblong panel above the miniature describing the framed scene below: "But the Lord hurled the Egyptians into the sea" (Exodus 14:27); "But the Israelites marched through the sea on dry ground" (Exodus 14:29). The practice of placing explanatory inscriptions in panels or frames above or below the miniatures is already encountered in ninth-century Carolingian miniatures and continued in thirteenth-century Latin manuscripts. The Hebrew writing in the margin is by a later hand, and, for the most part, simply repeats the barely legible panel inscriptions. In the frame, a running chevron band pattern with alternating blue and orange colors appears between two interrupted fret designs. Triple tendrils shoot from the corners of the frame. The blue and orange colors are again used for the *Crossing of the Israelites,* thereby effectively integrating both frame and pictorial composition. Five bands are shown; three with blue undulating lines to indicate the Red Sea underneath which are visible the drowning Egyptians, their horses, and armor. Between two orange bands—indicating dry land—we see the columns of Israelites marching across. The depiction of the Hebrews crossing the Red Sea in either straight paths or in concentric semi-circles is a legendary embellishment that we can trace back to a Dura-Europos synagogue painting of the third century. According to legend, God prepared twelve paths at the Red Sea—one for each tribe. Byzantine and later Western Christian art are familiar with this extra-biblical interpretation. Similarly, we note that the Israelites are shown as armed soldiers crossing the Red Sea. The uncertain Hebrew word *hamushim* (Exodus 13:18) was interpreted by the rabbis to mean that the Israelites went up armed out of Egypt. This legendary motif is again in the Dura painting and in most *Sephardi Haggadot.* It is also found in the eleventh-century *Farfa Bible* (Rome: Vatican Library, Ms. lat. 5729, fol. 82).

PLATE 14

RYLANDS HAGGADAH

fol. 19v *Celebration of Passover*

Divided horizontally, this miniature has three box-like interiors with the front cut away. The interior spatial techniques, introduced by such Italian masters as Duccio and Giotto, had reached Spain by the second quarter of the fourteenth century. The decorative banding below the ceiling is familiar from Romanesque Italian churches; later adaptations appear in Catalonian architecture. Similarly, the figure style—the small stocky figures placed within spacious interiors—reveals the Italo-Gothic style which came to dominate Spanish art during much of the fourteenth century. These miniatures may have been painted in a Valencian workshop in the second quarter of the fourteenth century, as they show stylistic affinities to a manuscript in the Cathedral of Valencia (*Epistolario,* No. 58). Below the Hebrew inscription—"a lamb to a family" (Exodus 12:3); "They shall take some of the blood and put it on the doorposts" and "[they shall eat the lamb] roasted over the fire" (Exodus 12:7)—we note reading right to left, in keeping with the direction of the Hebrew script, a figure slaughtering a lamb, placing its blood on the doorposts with a hyssop, and roasting the lamb over a spit, as its flesh was to be consumed the same night. Below are two scenes of a contemporary Spanish Passover *Seder* celebration. On the right, an old bearded man is seated at a table, which is covered with a white tablecloth, and provided with a knife and the prescribed *matzot* (unleavened bread). He is raising a cup of wine with one hand and holding a closed book, the *Haggadah,* in the other, while a small figure, probably a servant, fills a cup. (Four cups are required for the entire ceremonial.) On the left we see a young couple also seated before a table spread with a white tablecloth. The husband raises the wine cup; a servant, wine decanter in hand, is about to fill another cup. Along with the *matzot,* we note a container apparently filled with stalks of celery. The couple is munching these celery stalks, which, according to *Sephardi* ritual, represent the *maror* (the bitter herbs), a symbol of the bitterness of slavery in Egypt. Like most others in the *Rylands Haggadah,* this miniature is so similar in format, iconography, and style to another fourteenth-century Spanish *Haggadah* (London: British Library, Ms. Or. 1404) that it may come from the same workshop—or both manuscripts may be based on the same model.

שה לבית אבת שה
לבית
ולקחו מן הדם ונתנו
על שתי המזוזת
צלי אש

PLATE 16

SARAJEVO HAGGADAH

fol. 30 *Revelation at Sinai*

The theophany at Sinai—the covenant revelation between God and Israel—is no doubt the most dramatic moment in Jewish history. For this scene the artist uses the full-page format. Moses stands isolated, engulfed by flames, holding the rounded, golden tablets in his hand. In keeping with the Exodus account (Chapter 19), a *shofar,* emerging from the clouds, appears to be blasting God's divine words into Moses's ear: "a dense cloud upon the mountain, a very loud blast of the horn." The figure holding the small tablets to the left may be Joshua or Aaron. Tightly encircling the small mountain are the Israelites. Here the artist attempted to create a crowd scene by showing full-view figures in the foreground and only heads in the background, an artistic device already encountered in Roman Imperial art. The central figure in a blue hooded garment with his back towards the audience leads the eye upwards to the ceremonial elevation of Moses. All the Israelites gaze upwards for the "people trembled" (Exodus 19:16) and, following the inscription, the Israelites vowed that "All that the Lord has spoken we will do!" (Exodus 19:8).

Heinrich Heine in his *Confessions* aptly captured the essence of the Sarajevo miniature: "How small Sinai appears when Moses stands upon it!" Contrasting Moses's accomplishments with those of the Greeks, Heine remarked that Moses was indeed a great artist who built human pyramids and carved human beings in order to create Israel.

Undoubtedly made for a Jewish artistocrat, the *Haggadah* miniatures carry out the prescription of the Spanish Jewish scholar Profiat Duran, who wrote in the early fifteenth century: "One should always study in beautiful and handsome books, whose elegant script is on fine vellum and whose adornments and bindings are resplendent" (*Ma'ase Efod,* 19).

PLATE 15

SARAJEVO HAGGADAH
fol. 29 *Israelites in the Desert*

The *Sarajevo Haggadah* was the first Hebrew manuscript to be reproduced in a facsimile edition. It appeared in 1898 with a scholarly commentary written by the well-known Viennese art historian Julius von Schlosser, and again in 1963 with another commentary; it has thus become the best-known Hebrew illuminated manuscript.

The full-page miniatures preceding the text are placed within a blue-red frame with white *rinceaux* decoration. These miniatures, painted on the fleshy side of the vellum only with the reverse left blank, are for the most part divided horizontally and set against alternating blue and red diapered backgrounds. In subject matter, the *Sarajevo Haggadah* has the most extensive cycle of all Spanish *Haggadot*—ranging from scenes drawn from the Books of Genesis to Deuteronomy. Although many of its miniatures undoubtedly used contemporary Latin bibilical illuminations as models, there are some unique Jewish features in the cycle: a man sitting in repose on the seventh day of Creation (the Sabbath), or the substitution of rays and a hand for God, and Abraham, about to sacrifice his son Isaac with a knife, in keeping with Jewish tradition, rather than with the more customary sword *(gladium)* in Christian manuscripts. As the escutcheon of the Kingdom of Aragon prominently appears above the battlements in a design on folio 3 of the text, it has been assumed that the *Haggadah* came from Catalonia, perhaps even from Barcelona. Certainly the figures and drapery reveal the Italo-Gothic style so pervasive in fourteenth-century Catalonia. No agreement has been reached by scholars on dating this manuscript; it was probably made in Catalonia during the third quarter of the fourteenth century.

The miniature is divided horizontally. The top panel has a blue diapered background in front of which stand two stylized trees. To the right, with little indication of stage space, several figures are bending over. They are, as the inscription makes clear, gathering *manna,* "some much, some little" (Exodus 16:17). To the left, Aaron "has taken a jar" (Exodus 16:33) and, as directed, has placed *manna* in it. Below the Israelites "came to Elim, where there were 12 springs and 70 palm trees" (Exodus 15:27). The figure on the left, holding the rod, is probably Moses.

ומשה עלה אלהאלהים
מתן תורה
ויחרד כל העם

בעזרת מושיע וגואל
אתחיל ספר דניאל

בשנת

שלש למלכות יהויקים בא
נבוכד נצר וגו׳ וכי אפשר ל
אמר כן והלא הוא מלך בע״ש
בשנת ארבע למלכות יהויקים
ש׳ בשנה הרביעית ליהויקים
בן יאשיהו מלך יהודה היא
השנה הראשונה לנבוכד נצר
מלך בבל׳ ומה ת״ל בשנת שלש
אמרו׳ ויהי לו יהויקים עבד
שלש שנים וישב וימרד בו׳
ומרד בו שלש שנים׳ ובשנת
שלש עלה עליו׳ והיו שנת
שמונה לנבוכד נצר ראשו׳ ומר
שנה ראשונה כבש נינוה ב׳
שנייה עלה וכבש יהויקים׳
ושלש שנים עבדו׳ ושלש ש״נ
שנים מרד בו׳ ומקצת כלי בית
האלהים׳ ומקצתן נשיירו ל
מה שנ׳ בירמיה כה אמר ייי צב׳
אל העמודים ואל הים ואל המכו׳
המכונות ואל יתר הכלים אש
אשר לא הגלה נבוכד נצר וגו׳
ויביאם ארץ שנער׳ בית אל
אלהיו׳ לקיים לעז׳ שלו הביא
את השביה מלה׳ אל׳ האנש׳
האנשים ואת הכלים הביא ל
בית האוצר׳ הפרתמים׳ רוב׳
רומסים׳ ואשר כח בהם לעמ׳

רבותינו

פירשו שמעמידין עצמן כש
כשמצרכין לנקביהם׳ ולאמרם
ספר׳ ומסב על אשר נח כתם
ומזן׳ לשון תורה׳ פת בג׳ הד׳
הוא שם ומאכל המלך בלשון ל
משרים׳ כך הוא מתמשע׳

ויש פותרים

פת בגם המלך ונותן להם ורב׳
ודעתם׳ ומזן ודעתם חלופי
להם׳ אלא חלופי הבשיל׳ בלש
בלשינר׳ על שם עצ׳ של בבל
הקרויה בל׳ שנ׳ ושריה מל׳
בלשער כשם אלהיה׳ יתגיל׳
לשון למלוך׳ שם הפריסים
שהוא שר על משרתי המלך
אשר מנה׳ אשר המזן ופסק
מנכם׳ ומגאתכם׳ והו מתמשע׳

ולשון משנה

הוא בן גלו׳ וחייבתם את ר״א
ראשי היו גוררים לו להתחי׳
להתחייב הנה ראשי׳ המלצר
שממונה על פי המגנים שב״נ
שבבית׳ שישקל בלשון לע׳
נס מי׳ לשון מפיון מן הזרעים
הזרעונים׳ וכאשר תראה לפי
מה שתראה עשה׳ עשיו את
פת בג׳ שלא לטמאו׳ אשר אמ׳
אמר המלך להביאם׳ שיבאו
לפני החרטומים שמשאילים
בטיורי המות׳ בעצמות המת
כמה ראות׳ אמר שחוק מדין
האשפים׳ אלו שמחקים את
את המזלות בכשפיהם׳

כך מפורש כא״

במדרש תנחומ׳

ויהי דניאל׳ בגדולה בבבל עד
שנת למלכות כורש׳ ודברי ה׳
המאמר הזה זה דניאל ומרד׳
נקראו שזה הוא שחתכוהו מג׳
מגדולתו׳ צריכין אנו לומר שזה
כורש הראשון שלפני אחשור׳
אחשורוש׳ ולדברי המאמר נ״ל
שכל דברי מלכות נחתכין על
פיו מאמר כורש זה הוא דריוש
השיני שאחר אחשורוש בי״מ
בימי דריוש המדי שהשליטו
שהשליטוהו לגוב אריות ולא
ירד מגדולתו שנ׳ ודניאל ועד
העלה במלכות דריוש ובמלכות
כורש פרסיה׳ ואירע שיוג׳ ל
בימי כורש השיני היה בגדולה׳
ובשנת שתים לנבוכד נצר חלם׳
אפשר לומר כן אלא בשנת
שתים לחורבן הבית׳

כ[illegible]א שנ־י

בסדר עולם׳ ד

ונקראו מלכות נבוכד נצר על

PLATE 17

Commentary to the Bible

Volume II, fol. 209 *Three Hebrews in the Fiery Furnace*

This biblical illumination comes from a predominantly Rashi commentary to the Bible made in the neighborhood of Würzburg around 1233. It is the oldest extant Hebrew illuminated manuscript from Germany.

The initial word panel carries the Hebrew word *bishnat*—the opening word of the verse in the book of Daniel—"*In the* third *year* of the reign . . ." On the right, four figures are kneeling, raising joined hands toward a huge figure of gold with gold crown, standing on a pedestal—a reference to the adoration of the golden idol erected in the valley of Dura by order of King Nebuchadnezzar (Daniel 3:7). Separated by a slender gold column, we note two groups of figures —on the right, a diminutive crowned figure with scepter in hand; behind him four larger figures, one supporting himself on a large sword while peering ahead with right hand over his forehead, the other brandishing a lance and turning his head toward the open vaulted furnace on the left. Amidst the flames shooting from the fiery furnace, four men are visible. (The features of these figures may have been scratched out later for pietistic reasons.) The illustration closely follows the biblical narrative (Daniel 3:21ff.), which refers to the three Hebrews who were cast into the fiery furnace bound by their clothing. Nebuchadnezzar is astonished to see the central, dignified fourth figure in this miniature, distinguished from the others by his long embroidered robe. The figure, according to the Bible, is in appearance "like a son of the gods"—the divine messenger who protected the three Hebrews (Daniel 3:24ff.). The short stature of King Nebuchadnezzar can perhaps be explained by a Jewish legendary embellishment of the story which suggests that Nebuchadnezzar did not enjoy life because of his dwarfish figure.

The scene is quite common in Christian art and is already found in the catacombs; it is rare, however in Hebrew manuscripts (Cf. London: British Library, Ms. Add. 11639, fol. 259v, another illustration of this theme in a Hebrew book, which is unrelated iconographically). Acquired in the sixteenth century by the banker Johann Jakob Fugger, this miniature, as Hanns Swarzenski has shown, belongs to a group of late Romanesque Latin manuscripts emanating from the vicinity of Würzburg.

PLATE 18

Schocken Bible

fol. 1v *Frontispiece to Genesis*

Set against a light blue background are forty-six roundels surrounding the initial word panel *bereshit*—the opening word of the Book of Genesis. The alternating blue and red colors of the roundels were, of course, favorite colors of stained glass windows and are found in contemporary Christian manuscripts (for example, Kremsmünster, Stiftsbibliothek, Cod. 243). Such decorative motifs as the composite flowers seen from above and the short stout figures seem to point to the art of southwest Germany in the early fourteenth century. The iconography of the roundels depends upon Christian biblical cycles of the period, although some Jewish legendary material is introduced.

Reading from right to left: First row: 1. Adam and Eve and the serpent. 2. Expulsion from paradise. 3. Cain slays Abel. 4. Noah's Ark. 5. Noah pruning his vine. 6. Tower of Babel. Second row: 7. Destruction of Sodom and Gomorrah. 8. Sacrifice of Isaac. 9. Isaac blesses Jacob. 10. Esau returns from the hunt. 11. Jacob's dream at Bethel. 12. Jacob wrestles with the angel. Third row: 13–14. The two dreams of Joseph. 15. Joseph meets the angel Gabriel (an extra-biblical legend). 16. Joseph's brethren tending their flocks. 17. Joseph stripped of his coat. 18. Joseph sold to Ishmaelites. Fourth row: 19. Joseph and Potiphar's wife. 20. The baker's and butler's dreams. Fifth row: 21. Joseph interpreting their dreams. 22. Pharaoh's dreams. Sixth and seventh row: 23. Joseph interpreting Pharaoh's dream. 24. Joseph as viceroy of Egypt. 25–31. Joseph and his brethren. 32–33. Slavery in Egypt (?). 34. Discovery of infant Moses. Pharaoh's daughter's hand is miraculously lengthened (legend). Eighth row: 35. Pharaoh's daughter gives Moses to his mother. 36–37. Moses and the burning bush. 38. Moses and Aaron before Pharaoh. 39. The Exodus. 40. Moses divides the Red Sea. Ninth row: 41. Drowning of Egyptians. 42. Miriam and the women of Israel celebrate. 43. Theophany at Sinai. 44. Spies carry grapes from Canaan. 45. Korah and company swallowed (?). 46. Balaam and his ass.

18

19

PLATE 19

Pentateuch

fol. 238 *Frontispiece to Deuteronomy*

The dark blue panel within the elaborate architectural framework has the gold letters of the Hebrew word *eleh* ("*these* are the words"), which begins the Book of Deuteronomy. Were it not for the Hebrew word, it would be difficult to tell the difference between this page and those from German Latin manuscripts of the fourteenth century.

Written on fine vellum, this manuscript at one time belonged to the Duke of Sussex. Its vibrant colors of blue, purple, red, yellow, and green and the expressive grotesqueries resemble the style of the artists who worked on such south German manuscripts as the 1310 *Aich Bible* (Kremsmünster, Stiftsbibliothek, Cod. 351–354). The architectural background is an adaptation of large-scale churches in Germany with a stepped-in brick gable above the nave. The lancet windows are handled in a fanciful way. Below the Hebrew word is a six-pointed star in gold, surrounded by animal grotesques, and within the red roundel in the center of the star is an elephant (probably modeled after a depiction in a Bestiary). The six-pointed star (*Magen David*—the shield of David, but also known as the Seal of Solomon in the Middle Ages) is a symbol now linked almost exclusively with Judaism and Zionism. In the Middle Ages, however, the *Magen David* had little intrinsic Jewish significance, but was known and used as a magical symbol in both Christianity and Islam.

PLATE 20

Miscellany

fol. 117v *David Playing the Harp*

Framed and set against a blue diapered background is "David playing his harp." He is seated on a chair and is wearing a light orange royal cloak lined with ermine. Above his crowned and youthful head is a cusped arch with pinnacle forms. The miniature itself, part of a large cycle of mainly biblical images, is placed between the text of the Psalms written in the lower margins of folios 14v–113v and 124–158v. David playing his harp is an old motif; it is already encountered in a painting in the third-century Dura-Europos synagogue and in a Gaza synagogue mosaic pavement, dated 509. This miniature, however, most closely resembles twelfth- and thirteenth-century English and French Psalter miniatures, where a seated, crowned David is frequently featured.

The paintings in this manuscript were executed by several hands; most were painted in the last quarter of the thirteenth century and some in the first quarter of the fourteenth. The David miniature probably belongs to the first hand and may date around 1280–1290. The style of the elegant figure—its hair and facial expression—is very close to the late work emanating from what Robert Branner has called the "Aurifaber atelier." The French origin of this miniature is further attested to by the frequent mention of French rabbis by Benjamin, the principal scribe of the entire manuscript—for example, Rabbi Hezekiah of Troyes (fol. 242) and Rabbi Jehiel of Paris (fol. 252). Again, were it not for the Hebrew inscription at the bottom of this miniature, we would be hard put to distinguish it from similar ones in Latin Christian manuscripts of the period.

זה דוד המנגן בנבל

PLATE 21

Miscellany

fol. 523v *David and Goliath*

Made by the second and more skilled artist, and dating from the end of the thirteenth century, the beautifully painted and composed encounter of David and Goliath is placed against a light red diapered background within a roundel framed by a gold band. This miniature, like many others in the manuscript, is not directly connected with any of its texts, and its inscription, "this is Goliath, the Philistine," may have been added later.

The contest between David and Goliath, a favorite subject of Byzantine and later Western Psalter iconography, is encountered only infrequently in Hebrew manuscripts. The towering, armed figure of Goliath dominates the miniature. Holding his blue and gold shield with his right hand and his huge lance, whose shaft and tip break through the roundel frame, with his left, he faces the diminutive David. The strong contrast between the blue of David's plain garment and Goliath's adorned shield is most effective. Goliath is hiding behind his large shield which menacingly points toward David. Bravely confronting Goliath, David is armed only with a sling and is surrounded by rams and sheep who pasture by his side. A small barking dog is between the combatants. Close analogies to this miniature can be found in David and Goliath scenes in the *Pierpont Morgan Picture Bible* (New York: Pierpont Morgan Library, Ms. 638, fol. 28v) and the *Breviary of Phillippe le Bel* (Paris: Bibl. Nat., Ms. lat. 1023, fol. 1v)—both High Gothic manuscripts from the second half of the thirteenth century. We need only compare the flat helmet and the armor of Goliath in this miniature with that in the Morgan painting, and David's swaying figure and finely modeled drapery to the depiction in the *Breviary,* to be persuaded of the Parisian models or inspiration of our artist.

זה גלית הפלשתי
ודוד הזורק לו
וכלבו והאילים סביבו

PLATE 22

PENTATEUCH

fol. 104v *Micrographic Frontispiece to Leviticus*

Entirely done in micrography, this stylized design shows three cusped arches surmounted by straight-sided gables, which are topped by foliated motifs and separated by pinnacle forms. An adaptation of a porch extending out from the portal of such south German cathedrals as Regensburg, the micrographic pen drawings of the Masoretic notes have a red stippled background.

Resting upon a band of six roundels which have floral and animal inserts is the central arch carrying the initial Hebrew word, *vayikra* ("The Lord *called* . . ."), the opening word of the book of Leviticus. The Hebrew letter *alef,* at the end of the word *vayikra,* is traditionally written in smaller script. Decorated by the scribe Moses of Ebermannstadt (near Bamberg, Bavaria), it is likely that the manuscript dates from the early fourteenth century (the date 1290 in the colophon is by another hand). The use of micrography in Germany probably began in the twelfth century as Judah ben Samuel he-Hasid of Regensburg proscribed the practice in his *Sefer Hasidim,* 709: "He who employs a scribe to write the twenty-four books [i.e., the Hebrew Bible] should do so only on the condition that the scribe will not shape the masoretic notes in the form of birds or beasts or similar things."

Jewish scribes, despite the admonition, saw no anomaly in twisting the *masorah,* which served both as a guide and guardian of the text, into the form of birds, beasts, and human beings, even though this made the writing difficult to read.

PLATE 23

Mishneh Torah of Maimonides

fol. 46v *Frontispiece, Book II*

The initial word panel reads *sefer sheni,* the second of the fourteen-book legal code, *Mishneh Torah*—Maimonides's *summa theologica.* Called the *Book of Love,* it deals with love of God, prayers, phylacteries, priestly blessings, and circumcision. The gracefully curling tendrils within the word panel send forth their shoots from the vine scroll decoration to cover and frame the entire page. Standing on the tendril in the upper margin, a man shoots an arrow at the exposed hindquarters of another man—one of many such *obscaena* found in the margins of thirteenth- and fourteenth-century Gothic manuscripts from England and the Franco-Flemish provinces which Lilian Randall studied.

At the bottom of the page is another familiar medieval scene: a fox with a cock in his jaws is being chased by an irate woman with a distaff and spindle in her right hand. The anecdote of the cock—symbolic of a vain and pompous character—belongs to the realm of medieval *exempla* by which the mendicant Franciscans and, in particular, the Dominicans embellished their sermons while preaching in the vernacular. This scene is unconnected with the text, and one wonders whether Jewish preachers of the period also resorted to these anecdotes in their sermons.

It has been assumed that the manuscript, written by Nathan ben Simeon ha-Levi for his brother-in-law, Rabbi Abraham ben Rabbi Berakhiah, in 1295–1296, came from Cologne, since corrections and explanations of the text were made in that city by another scribe in 1413. Stylistically, however, the miniatures bear little relation to German Gothic manuscripts of the period, but we do find stylistic and iconographic affinities to a group of Gothic manuscripts made in the Cambrai region in the late thirteenth and fourteenth centuries. The four-volume manuscript, which deserves further scrutiny, also has some biblical *bas de pages* illustrations, such as Adam and Eve and the Sacrifice of Isaac—these, too, unrelated to the text. It is only in Italy in the fourteenth and fifteenth centuries that we find editions of the *Mishneh Torah* with illustrations of the contents of the legal text itself (Figures XVII–XVIII).

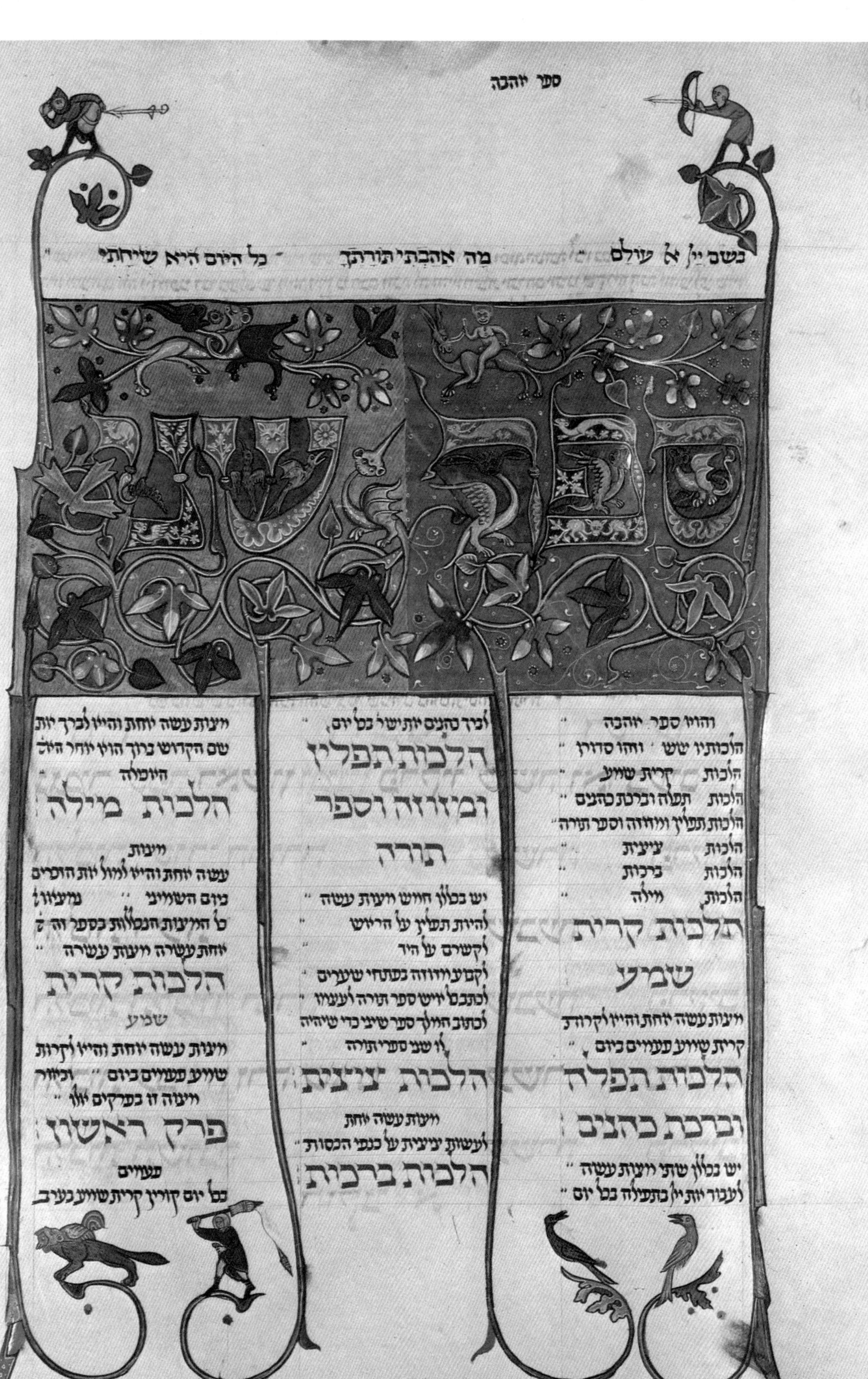

ספר אהבה

בשם יי׳ אל עולם — מה אהבתי תורתך — כל היום היא שיחתי

והוא ספר אהבה
הלכותיו שש וזהו סדורן
הלכות קרית שמע
הלכות תפלה וברכת כהנים
הלכות תפלין ומזוזה וספר תורה
הלכות ציצית
הלכות ברכות
הלכות מילה

הלכות קרית שמע

מצות עשה אחת והיא לקרות
קרית שמע פעמים ביום

הלכות תפלה וברכת כהנים

יש בכללן שתי מצות עשה
לעבוד את יי׳ בתפלה בכל יום
ולברך כהנים את ישראל בכל יום

הלכות תפלין ומזוזה וספר תורה

יש בכללן חמש מצות עשה
להיות תפלין על הראש
ולקשרם על היד
ולקבוע מזוזה בפתחי שערים
ולכתוב כל איש ספר תורה לעצמו
ולכתוב המלך ספר שני כדי שיהיה
לו שני ספרי תורה

הלכות ציצית

מצות עשה אחת
לעשות ציצית על כנפי הכסות

הלכות ברכות

מצות עשה אחת והיא לברך את
שם הקדוש ברוך הוא אחר הא׳
האכילה

הלכות מילה

מצות
עשה אחת והיא למול את הזכרים
ביום השמיני נמצאו
כל המצות הנכללות בספר זה
אחת עשרה מצות עשה

הלכות קרית שמע

מצות עשה אחת והיא לקרות
שמע פעמים ביום וביאור
מצוה זו בפרקים אלו

פרק ראשון

פעמים
בכל יום קורין קרית שמע בערב

PLATE 24

LEIPZIG MAHZOR

Volume I, fol. 51v *Hanging of Haman and his Sons (Purim)*

Hanging by a rope from the branches of a tall tree are eleven figures whose eyes are bound with cloths. In the lower left-hand margin a woman with long, blond hair lies prostrate, her hands uplifted towards the tree. Further left, a man leads a blue horse with a golden saddle on which sits a crowned figure in green garb; a medieval Jew's hat *(pileus cornutus)* is suspended from a strap on his back. Behind the rider is a red watch tower with Gothic door and windows and blue roof tiles from which a woman pours a greenish liquid on the figure leading the horse. The scene accompanies the *piyyut* for the *Purim* holiday, beginning with "and they hung Haman." Based on Jewish legendary elaborations on the Book of Esther, Haman's daughter is shown pouring the contents of a chamber pot over her father's head as he leads Mordecai on the king's horse. The prostrate figure is again Haman's daughter who, realizing that she has defiled her father and not Mordecai, commits suicide by jumping from the tower window. The figures hanging from the tree branches are Haman and his ten sons.

As has been demonstrated, the miniatures in this *mahzor* come from an Upper Rhenish workshop and date from the first quarter of the fourteenth century. The dark outlines emphasizing the drapery folds, the short figures with small rounded heads, the long, loosely belted dress with its tight sleeves, and the vivid color contrasts bear close stylistic resemblance to such contemporary Christian manuscripts as the *Rudolf of Ems World Chronicle* (St. Gall: Stadtbibliothek, Cod. 312), made in the Lake Constance region.

ויתלו את המן

PLATE 25

Leipzig Mahzor

Volume II, fol. 164v *Abraham in the Fire (Yom Kippur)*

Within a tabernacle form made up of columns terminating in pinnacles, we note straight side gables which are topped by foliate motifs and crenelation. The interior tear-drop tracery forms in the columns are reminiscent of windows found in German hall churches. Under the compressed arches over the Hebrew text is the *piyyut* for the *minhah* (afternoon) service of *Yom Kippur* (Day of Atonement) praising Abraham as the first believer in the One God and recounting his many trials—"Abraham, our steadfast forbear, discerned Your faithfulness in an age when man knew not Your will."

At the bottom of the page is a Jewish legend recounting Abraham's rescue from the fire of the Chaldeans by divine intervention. According to the *aggadic* elaborations, Abraham, at the insistence of his father Terah, was summoned to appear before King Nimrod after breaking all the idols in Terah's shop. A theological dispute followed, with Abraham refusing to recognize Nimrod, fire, or water as the Lord of the Universe; therefore he was consigned to the flames from which God Himself or an angel rescued him. To the left of our miniature a crowned Nimrod sits in judgment. In front of him is Terah, who is wearing an Eastern-type headdress and accusing Abraham, who stands next to him, along with his brother Haran (both depicted with the medieval Jew's hat). The prostrate figure before the throne may be the jailer who, according to legend, pleaded with Nimrod to save Abraham. Abraham, it appears, had been incarcerated for one year and was given neither food nor water, but somehow miraculously survived. The jailer knew this and pleaded with King Nimrod not to force him to kill this man who, through a miracle, was still alive. To the right we have Abraham, engulfed in flames, while the hand of God reaches down from the clouds to offer him salvation.

PLATE 26

Leipzig Mahzor

Volume II, fol. 181v *Leviathan and Behemoth (Sukkot)*

The foliated initial word panel has the opening Hebrew word *akhtir* ("*I will crown* with a wreath of praise . . .") of the *piyyut* recited during the morning service of the first day of *Sukkot* (Tabernacles). Next to the decorated panel we see a Jew wearing the prescribed medieval Jew's hat and holding the symbols of the holiday, a *lulov* (palm branch) and *etrog* (a citrus fruit). This figure, like most others in the manuscript, is shown in profile with a rounded eagle's beak. There is no mouth or nose, only the hint of a mouth in the downward curve of the beak. This artistic convention of attaching animal heads to human figures was prevalent in southern German Hebrew illuminations from the second half of the thirteenth to the early fourteenth centuries.

In the lower margin are a large blue-scaled fish with open mouth—Leviathan—and a raging, reddish brown bull—Behemoth. According to rabbinic tradition, God will command these mythical beasts to engage in mortal combat: "Behemoth will, with its horns, pull Leviathan down and rend it, and Leviathan will, with its fins, pull Behemoth down and pierce it through" (*Leviticus Rabbah* 13:3). The struggle of Leviathan and Behemoth is depicted in several late thirteenth- and early fourteenth-century German Hebrew manuscripts because the *Sukkot* liturgy and rabbinic texts express the fervent hope that God will use Leviathan's skin to construct a *sukkah* (booth or tent) and prepare Leviathan and Behemoth's meat for the banquet of the righteous dead in messianic times.

אז התהלה לנורא עלילה

במי זאת עלה באדר תנים בעלסה גנת תנים אעלסה
למלך רם ונשא גדתי ארבע במספר רובע לחן על
ארבע אסלד בשבח והודה בתוך
קהל עדה בלוקחי להב ואגודה קדוש

ידרש במו צדק לשופטם בצדק דינם להדינא לצדקה
הלל כם אפנה ומליצי ירנה וסוהב אנא ורוכן בפתרון
יכוש יחטא בצל תכבוש קראתיך אל אכוש

זכר סיכוך להורות להם להורות לסכך
ולקרות חסות בצל סוכה מחוק נסוכה שבעה להסתוכבה
טילול ענים אזכירה בכל דור ודור אזכרה לחסדי ה
דוד זכרה יקב סוכתו ויכון מלכותו והרב
גדולתו כימי עולם ומלכותו עד העולם לדוד ולזרעו עד

27

PLATE 27

MAHZOR

fol. 3 *Revelation at Sinai (Shavuot)*

The gold Hebrew letters of the word *adon* begin the liturgical poem for *Shavuot* (Pentecost)—"*The Lord* has taken care of me." According to rabbinic tradition, *Shavuot* is linked with God's giving the Torah (the books of Moses) to Israel at Mount Sinai. This dramatic event is rendered in our large *mahzor*. A beardless Moses reverently kneels on the slope of Mount Sinai in order to receive the rectangular tablets inscribed with the opening words of the Ten Commandments. [Decalogue tablets with rounded tops—today a commonplace—first appeared in an eleventh-century English Hexateuch (London: British Library, Ms. Claudius B. IV).] Behind Moses stands a mitred Aaron, hands folded in prayer. A little further off stand seven Jews with the pointed medieval Jews' hats; behind them a group of animal-headed, praying women are gazing piously upwards. Trumpets and *shofars* emerge from the clouds, alluding to the biblical passage, "the whole mountain trembled violently" and "the blare of the *shofar* grew louder and louder" (Exodus 19:18–19). This manuscript is the second volume of a tripartite *mahzor* (Volume I is in Budapest: Library of the Hungarian Academy of Sciences, Kaufmann Collection, Ms. A 384; and Volume III is in Oxford: Bodleian Library, Ms. Mich. 619). The figure style of the miniatures in the tripartite *mahzor* can be compared to a group of south German Latin manuscripts dating from the first quarter of the fourteenth century. The puffed-out hair and vivid colors, the soft undulation of the garment folds, and the flat ornamental treatment of floral elements are reminiscent of such manuscripts as the early fourteenth-century gradual of Saint Katharienthal (Zürich: Schweizerisches Landesmuseum, Ms. 128).

ויהי

[illegible]

בימי שפט השפטים ויהי רעב בארץ
וילך איש מבית לחם יהודה לגור בש
בשדי מואב הוא ואשתו ושני בניו
ושם האיש אלימלך ושם אשתו נעמי
ושם שני בניו מחלון וכליון אפרתים
מבית לחם יהודה ויבאו שדי מואב
ויהיו שם וימת אלימלך איש נעמי
ותשאר היא ושני בניה וישאו להם
נשים מאביות שם האחת ערפה ושם
השנית רות וישבו שם כעשר שנים
וימותו גם שניהם מחלון וכליון ותשאר
האשה משני ילדיה ומאישה ותקם
היא וכלתיה ותשב משדי מואב כי ש
שמעה בשדה מואב כי פקד יהוה את

PLATE 28

MAHZOR

fol. 71 *Ruth and Boaz (Shavuot)*

On either side of a series of cusped arches are stylized medieval fortification towers. The composition itself is divided by two trees whose heavy blossoming branches are spread over the blue ground. On the right is the Hebrew word *vayehi* ("and it came to pass . . ."), the opening word of the Book of Ruth read during the morning service of the second day of the *Shavuot* (Pentecost) festival.

Unlike the Scroll of Esther, which received lavish ornamentation and illustrations from the late sixteenth century onward, the Scroll of Ruth has only a few isolated scenes in Hebrew manuscripts (cf., for instance, a pen drawing, dating probably from fifteenth-century Germany in the *Worms Mahzor,* Jerusalem: Jewish National and University Library, Ms. Hebr. 4° 781/II, fol. 35). On the right-hand side, an animal-headed Ruth, sickle in hand, is found gleaning amidst four figures, one with a rake and another binding the sheaves. Ruth appears to have a cat's head, and the other figure, who may be Boaz (?), is shown with an ass's head. This scene may refer to Ruth 2:15–16, where Boaz admonishes his people to "let her glean even among the sheaves, and do not reproach her. And also pull out some from the bundles for her. . . ." Identification of the biblical characters is difficult since a similar figure with ass's head and wearing an identical garment is found among the women in the previous miniature (Plate 27). On the left-hand side, Ruth, hands folded, appears to be conversing with two male threshers of the harvest.

These richly decorated rectangular panels in the tripartite *mahzor* are closely related, both in script and style, to the miniatures in a group of Hebrew manuscripts—all probably made in south Germany during the first quarter of the fourteenth century (cf. London: British Library, Ms. Add. 15282 and Vienna Österreichische Nationalbibliothek, Cod. Hebr. 75). Why only certain figures were singled out for animal heads in this manuscript deserves further investigation.

PLATE 29

Darmstadt Haggadah

fol. 48v *Decorative Page*

Prominently centered is the panel carrying the golden letters of the Hebrew word *az,* the beginning of the *piyyut*—"how many the wonders you have wrought"—recited from the *Haggadah* on the first night of Passover. The Hebrew text is surrounded by a rich architectural frame consisting of several stories of Gothic details divided into niche-like compartments with either standing or seated figures within them. The lower part focuses on a woman dressed in a deep blue garment with veiled headdress; the upper part is centered around a young man with an open book on his lap. The triple arcade below and the five part arcade above draw the various figural groups together.

This miniature, like most others in this famous *Darmstadt Haggadah,* is almost totally divorced from the Hebrew text and reveals few iconographic parallels to medieval *Haggadot.* Were this scene to be found in a Christian manuscript, the bearded old man on top with a closed book in his right hand would be interpreted as God, the Father, with Christ, the Son, teaching below. The seated woman in the lower part pointing out passages in her book to the bearded Jew on the right would be identified as the Virgin. We know from the colophon (fol. 56v) that Israel ben Meir of Heidelberg was the scribe for this *Haggadah;* he did not illuminate it, as is frequently claimed. Since all Jews were expelled from Heidelberg in 1390 and there is no indication of Jewish ownership until the seventeenth century, is it possible that the loose folios of this *Haggadah* came into the hands of a wealthy Christian patron who, along with the illuminators and binder, had little or no knowledge of the Hebrew text and was also unacquainted with any tradition of *Haggadah* illuminations? This miniature reveals the Gothic International style in its sensitive use of color and the elegance of the loose and ample folds of the garments; it was probably painted by the master of an Upper Rhenish Christian workshop around 1430. Similar several-storied, fanciful architectural arrangements can be found in the surviving wall paintings in the church of Eriskirck, near Lake Constance, dated ca. 1410–1420. The slim, pointing hands and delicate, oval faces are stylistically close to the playing card figures in the Stuttgart Landesmuseum, made in the Upper Rhine region around 1427–1431.

רוב נסים הפלאת

PLATE 30

MISCELLANY

fol. 35v *The Messiah at the Passover Seder*

Next to the square blue *Ashkenazi* word *shefokh* ("*Pour out* Your wrath upon the nations that do not know You . . ."; Psalms 79:6 and Jeremiah 10:25), recited from the Passover *Haggadah* during the *Seder* ceremony, appears a fortified medieval city perched atop a mountain. From the openings of its towers and houses, figures peer out at the scene below. A man, arms outstretched, seems to be welcoming a crowned figure, garbed in red, blowing a *shofar* and riding upon an ass. This is Elijah-Messiah combined in one person. The ass and the crown are the attributes of the Messiah, while the *shofar* is traditionally linked with Elijah, the Messianic herald. The scroll above the standing figure testifies to this identification, for it reads: "Say to the daughter of Zion, behold your salvation comes . . ." (Isaiah 62:11). Additional testimony is supplied by the verses on the three scrolls placed around the three bearded half-figures who appear above the word *shefokh*. These verses, reading from right to left, are culled from such biblical books as Zechariah 9:9: "Rejoice greatly, O daughter of Zion. . . . Behold your king comes to you . . . humble and riding upon an ass . . ." (Micah 5:1 and Isaiah 43:1). In the lower margin, nude figures can still be made out emerging from their tombs—not too dissimilar from Last Judgment scenes in Gothic Christian art—to denote the resurrection of the dead, traditionally associated with the Messiah's coming.

This is the earliest instance of an iconographic convention found in about a dozen *Ashkenazi Haggadah* manuscripts—predominantly from the second half of the fifteenth century. This illustration depicts a Jewish custom, still in vogue today, of opening the door to greet the Messianic guest while the verses of *shefokh* are recited. Responding to omnipresent Palm Sunday processions, in which sculptured wooden images of Christ on his *Palmesel* were carried on carts to the gate of a mock Jerusalem, Jews asserted their traditional belief that the Messiah was yet to come. Furthermore, the persecutions and constant vilifications in fifteenth-century Germany demanded a much-needed escape—the fervent hope for the actual coming of the Messiah on the Night of Redemption (Passover). Hence, theological and socio-economic reasons alike prompted the emergence of these images in medieval *Ashkenazi Haggadot*.

PLATE 31

MISCELLANY

fol. 79 *Scenes of Martyrdom (Hanukkah)*

The unframed illustrations in this Hebrew Miscellany were probably planned by the scribe, Isaac ben Simhah Gansmann, who signed his name on folio 122, at the very beginning of a calendar commencing with the year 1428. Some of the depictions—unique to Hebrew iconography—appear here for the first time. Cases in point are the illustrations to the medieval *piyyut* for *Hanukkah* (Feast of Dedication or Lights)—an adaptation from the apocryphal Books II and IV Maccabees—which describe the martyrdom of the seven sons of a pious Jewish woman, usually identified in medieval Jewish sources as Hannah. (The Books of Maccabees were not canonized as part of the Hebrew Bible, but do belong to the Christian Old Testament canon.)

In the illustrations on this folio, the uppermost scene shows two women who, in defiance of the king's decree, have circumcised their sons. They are being suspended from a tree by their breasts in punishment; their children have been cast down from a medieval tower. Next, we see Eleazar, the high priest, whom the king is trying to persuade to offer false sacrifices. The ninety-year-old man has refused and, in the following scene, is about to be decapitated by a large sword. The bottom illustration shows the heroic martyrdom of the seven innocent brothers who are being burnt and mutilated because they refused to abandon their Lord and Creator and eat unlawful sacrifices commanded by the king.

Several hands worked on this manuscript—this folio belongs to the most naive and least sophisticated of the artists. Perhaps stemming from the Middle Rhine region from the second quarter of the fifteenth century, these illustrations reflect the more forceful linear renderings in pen and color tinting found in contemporary secular German folk manuscripts.

PLATE 32

HAGGADAH

fol. 7v *The Five Rabbis of Benei Berak*

This miniature illustrates the Passover *Haggadah* passage: "it happened once that [five sages] Rabbis Eliezer, Joshua, Eleazar ben Azaryah, Akiba and Tarfon reclined [around their *Seder* table] to discuss the Exodus from Egypt throughout the whole night." Here they are not reclining, but are standing around a lectern upon which lies an open book. The figure in a red garment points to the relevant passage under discussion. Written in square *Ashkenazi* script, this manuscript is probably the most controversial work in a large *oeuvre* attributed to an artist-scribe, Joel ben Simeon Ashkenazi, of Bonn or Cologne. The colophon in our manuscript (fol. 48v) reads: "My heart prompts me to answer him who might ask: Who designed this? I Feibush, called Joel, am the one [who designed this] for Jacob Mattathias. . . ."

The illumination and lavish decorations, the stocky, expressive and well-modeled figures, set within receding space, which appear on many folios do not accord with, however, the less-skilled, tinted Italianate drawings, scattered in the margins throughout the rest of the manuscript. The former illustrations are obviously south German and, as Sheila Edmunds has demonstrated, bear striking similarities in decoration and figure style to the workshop of Johannes Bämler of Augsburg who functioned as scribe, illuminator, and printer in the second half of the fifteenth century. Joel ben Simeon may have written this *Haggadah* in the 1460s and provided decorated initial word panels and some of the marginal illustration. The German owner, Jacob Mattathias (ben Isaac), perhaps turned the *Haggadah* over to Johannes Bämler. Bämler, as can still be noted in some folios, redid some of Joel's original designs and added other decorations and figures on folios 1v–8v and 39–46v. In some cases, as in this miniature, Bämler's decoration, around the initial Hebrew word panel, of blue scallops with semicircles of dots above the cusps, even encroaches on the Hebrew calligraphy. It should also be noted that Bämler illuminated folios in a *mahzor,* written around 1460 (Munich: Bayrische Staatsbibliothek, Cod. Hebr. 3/II).

הקב״ה את אבותינו ממצרים
הרי אנו בנינו ובני בנינו משעת
משעבדים היינו לפרעה במצ
במצרים ואפלו כלנו חכמים
כלנו נבונים כלנו זקנים כלנו
יודעים את התורה מצוה עלינו
לספר ביציאת מצרים המספר
ביציאת מצרים הרי זה משובח:
מעשה בר׳ אליעזר
ור׳ יהושע ור׳ טרפון
ור׳ אלעזר בן עזריה
ור׳ עקיבא שהיו מסבין בבני

PLATE 33

Arba'a Turim of Jacob ben Asher, Part II

Between fols. 127–128 *Slaughtering of Animals*

This is a frontispiece to the second part of the four-part *Arba'a Turim (Four Rows,* after the rows of jewels on the breastpiece of the High Priest, Exodus 28:17)—a law code written in the fourteenth century by Jacob ben Asher. The second section of the code is called *Yoreh De'ah (Teacher of Knowledge),* and deals with the laws concerning things lawful and unlawful. As it commences with the laws of *shehitah* (ritual slaughter) and *terefot* (ritually unclean), this framed illumination deals with these subjects.

In the background are two men slaughtering fowl and in front are two other men—one busy ritually slaughtering an ox; another probing the slaughtered ox to determine if it meets ritual specifications. A woman peering through an arched opening in the rear looks on. A checkered ceiling and uptilted brickwork floor are attempts to express depth. (A related scene can be found in a *Tur* in Rome: Biblioteca Casanatense, Ms. Ebr. Cod. 3096, fol. 1.) The wide and rich border decoration enfolding the miniature is composed of inhabited vine scrolls of putti, human figures, aster, columbine, cyclamen, and imaginary flowers. Written in cursive Italian Hebrew script by the scribe Isaac ben Obadiah in Mantua and completed on Thursday, November 24, 1435 for Rabbi Mordecai ben Avigdor, the miniature exhibits the refinement and delicacy so typical of the contemporary Gothic International style of Lombardy. The artist of the miniature reveals his indebtedness to such ateliers as those of the Zavattari brothers of Monza and Bonifacio Bembo of Cremona.

לא טוב

PLATE 34

Arba'a Turim of Jacob ben Asher, Part III

fol. 220 *Wedding*

The gold Hebrew words *lo tov* (*"it is not good* for man to be alone . . ."; Genesis 2:18) introduce the third part of the *Tur, Even ha-Ezer* (after "stone of help" mentioned in I Samuel 4:1). As this section deals with laws affecting women, especially marriage, divorce, legitimacy, etc., a wedding scene is introduced.

Arches spring from a slender pillar in the center and divide the scene in two. A triple frame of olive green, gold, and red encloses the miniature; the panel itself is surrounded by a widely ornamented border featuring barbed rosettes, strapwork design, animal, human, and *putti* figures. On the right-hand side of the panel, the bridal couple enters to the accompaniment of music. They are wearing extravagant and luxuriant headgear and garments trimmed with fur—typical features of the Gothic International style in Lombardy. On the left-hand side and in front of a green curtained backdrop, stand the assembled guests and the now bareheaded couple. The groom is placing the ring on the outstretched finger of the bride's right hand and is probably reciting the traditional formula: "Behold you are consecrated unto me with this ring, in accordance with the laws of Moses and Israel." Whether the officiant is joining the hands of the couple, as is the case in some other Italian Hebrew miniatures dating primarily from the second half of the fifteenth century, is difficult to tell (cf. *Rothschild Miscellany,* Jerusalem: Israel Museum, Ms. 180/51, fol. 120v; Budapest: Hungarian Academy of Sciences, Kaufmann Collection, Ms. 380/II, fol. 230, dated Pesaro, 1481; Parma: Biblioteca Palatina, Ms. Parm. 3596, fol. 275; Princeton: University Library, Garrett Ms. 26, fol. 13). The distinct Jewish wedding customs and ceremonies in Italy, as described in literature and depicted in art, are worthy of detailed study.

While the lively and elegantly accoutered figures are familiar from the Lombard Gothic style, they also reflect the general Renaissance indulgence in lavish dress to which the rich were given and which synods of Jewish communities, such as the one held at Forli in 1418, tried to prohibit by ordinance.

הפרק

הראשון מהלמוד
הראשון מהאופן הר
הראשון מהספר
הראשון בגדר
הרפואה

אומר

הרפואה

PLATE 35

Canon of Medicine of Avicenna, Book I

fol. 23v *Urinoscopy*

The miniature depicts a group of patients standing in the center of a spacious room carrying vessels containing urine specimens to a seated physician who holds up one vessel and points with his right hand. It introduces the chapter on urinoscopy—"Precautions necessary in collecting the urine, before forming an opinion as to its character"—of Nathan ha-Meati's Hebrew translation of Avicenna's famous eleventh-century *Canon of Medicine.*

In the left-hand and upper margins are twelve roundels carrying the twelve signs of the zodiac and the corresponding Labor of the Months. These may have been included, as Avicenna discusses the effect of changes of the seasons on the human body and what kind of diseases are peculiar to each climate. In the lower border, the three figures and, perhaps, the zodiacal roundel of the twins (*gemini*) may allude to Avicenna's four periods of life, with senility or decrepit age, seated in the center. Hebrew illuminated medical treatises are essentially found among Jews of fifteenth-century Italy. No other Hebrew manuscript of Avicenna's *Canon* is so splendidly illuminated. It was part of the booty carried to Paris in 1796 by Napoleon's army and was retrieved in 1815 after Napoleon's fall. Pietro Toesca tentatively assigned these miniatures to Leonardo da Besozzo, a judgment largely shared by Gian Alberto dell'Acqua and Mario Salmi, who is inclined to attribute the miniatures to a follower of Leonardo da Besozzo. There is no doubt that Lombard characteristics are present in the rich illuminations whose figures, set within minutely descriptive landscapes, ultimately recall Flemish tastes and influence. Mirella Levi D'Ancona, however, feels that, notwithstanding the obvious Lombard influences, the delicate colors and the feathery decorations of the miniatures may possibly be Venetian, as they resemble some manuscripts she has attributed to Cristoforo Cortese and his school.

PLATE 36

Sefer ha-Ikkarim of Joseph Albo, Book I

fol. 9 *Frontispiece*

Within a rich, deeply recessed landscape with castles and tall trees, three naked *putti* are upholding a cartouche carrying in gold Hebrew letters the opening word *yedi'at* ("*knowledge of* the fundamental principles upon which laws are based is both easy and difficult") of the first treatise of *Sefer ha-Ikkarim (Book of Principles),* a philosophic treatise on articles of faith by the fifteenth-century Spanish Jewish philosopher and preacher Joseph Albo.

Another cartouche, flanked by two winged, naked *putti,* appears above the clouds with *putto* heads. The verses written in cursive Italian Hebrew script are taken from Psalms 118:20: "This is the gate of the Lord; the righteous shall enter through it"; Psalms 36:12: "Let not the foot of pride overtake me, nor the hand of the wicked drive me away"; and Psalms 56:11: "In God, whose word I praise, in the Lord, whose word I praise. . . ." The splendidly illustrated framed panel is surrounded by an outer border of intricate white vine interlaces inhabited by a variety of animals, birds, centaurs, and naked *putti.* In the lower margin three *putti* surround a green wreath in which sits, set within the landscape, another naked *putto.* Profile busts of men and women are inserted in the roundels between the vines of the upper and outer margins. The use of *bianchi girari*—white vine scroll border decorations—was a standard feature of humanistic books and was adopted with regional variations all over Italy. It is not surprising, therefore, that it was employed for a Hebrew philosophical work, which probably comes from Florence and is attributed by Mirella Levi D'Ancona to the so-called "Uccellesque Master." He was a follower of Paolo Uccello and is not far in style from Ser Ricciardo di Nanni and Filippo de Matteo Torelli. We need only compare the delicate and subdued colors, the muscular *putti* with protruding stomachs, and the profile portrait heads to note the similarity to such manuscripts of Torelli as Josephus' *De Bello Judaico* (Florence: Laurentian Library, Plut. 66–69).

PLATE 37

Rothschild Miscellany
fol. 64v *Job*

Framed in gold is a Renaissance palazzo with one wing cut off on either side. Potted plants and human figures can be seen in the windows of the upper two stories of the building. The gold inscription in the scrolls above the palazzo comes from Job 42:10: *"and the Lord gave* Job twice as much as he had before."

Job, like a Renaissance prince, is seated within a niche of a portico with a rug spread under his feet. He points to his seven sons standing to the right; on his left, in keeping with the account of Job 42:13, are his three daughters. Folio 65, which continues the story of Job, also has a full-page miniature to show Job's wealth. Workers within an idyllic, rural setting are shown in his fertile fields, while in the foreground shepherds are tending Job's large flocks. This unique scene apparently emphasizes the fact that the Renaissance patron of the manuscript chose to identify with the Job whose faith and perseverance were rewarded, rather than the more customary depiction in both Jewish and Christian medieval manuscripts which presents a Job whom God has punished with severe afflictions. Many of the miniatures of this *Miscellany* were probably made in a workshop in the Ferrara region. Fanciful landscapes, brilliant colors, spatial perspective settings, and the precision of animal representations echo the style of such artists as Taddeo Crivelli who worked for the court of Este in the third quarter of the fifteenth century on such masterpieces as the *Bible of Borso d'Este* (Modena: Este Library, Ms. V. G. 12).

כל אשר

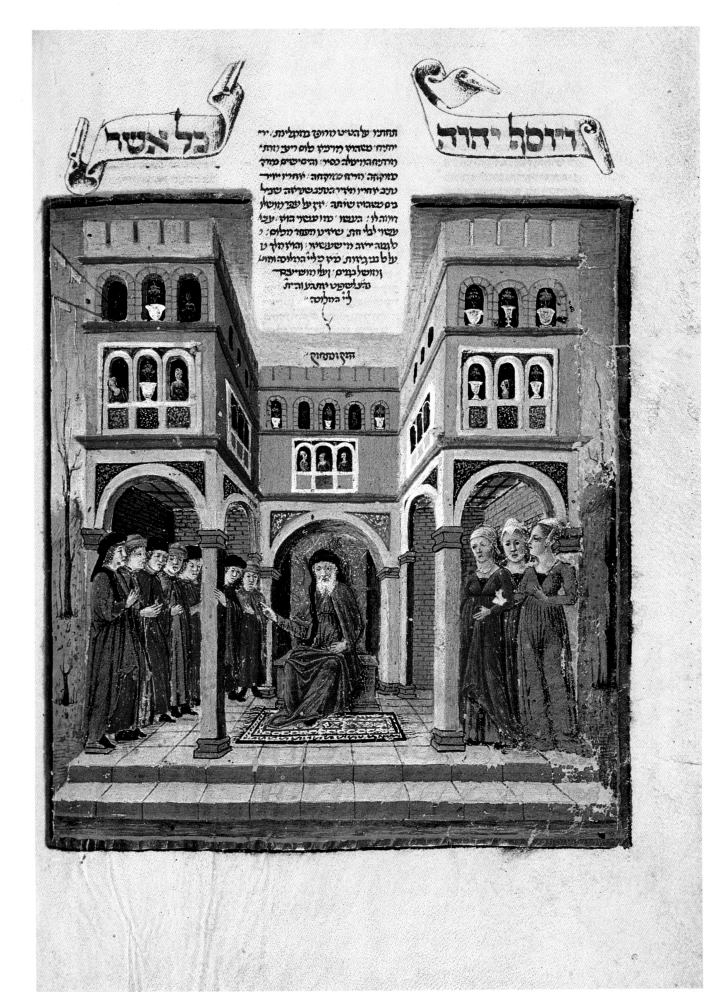

PLATE 38

Rothschild Miscellany

fol. 132v *Rosh ha-Shanah Page*

The illustration in the right upper margin has an old, bearded man wrapped in the *tallit* (the traditional prayer shawl) and standing before a lectern on which rests an open prayer book. A metal oil lamp is suspended from the vaulted room, and a blue brocaded cloth with fleur-de-lys motifs partitions the area to the left of the officiant. The reader is intoning the major theme of *Rosh ha-Shanah* (the Jewish New Year Holyday): "*Remember us* unto life, O king who delightest in life and inscribe us in the Book of Life." To the left of the framed inset we see in bold Hebrew letters the opening word of that pious wish, *zakhrenu*—"remember us"—set against a swirling background, strewn with delicate violets, exotic birds, animals, gilded knobs, and filigree ornamentation, as well as two children at play, one seated upon a reined fawn while the other follows behind him.

This so-called *Rothschild Miscellany* contains in its main and border texts more than forty religious and secular works. Among the religious books are Psalms, Proverbs, the Passover *Haggadah,* and the *mahzor.* The secular texts include such works as the Josippon history of the Jews (based on Josephus), and *Meshal ha-Kadmoni* by Isaac ibn Sahula (animal fables similar to those in the Arabic *Kalila and Dimna*). Profusely illuminated with over three-hundred illustrations, it is the most richly decorated Hebrew manuscript known. Stylistic differences in the manuscript point to an atelier where several artists undoubtedly worked on this sumptuous volume. No colophon exists, and only the name of Moses ben Yekutiel ha-Kohen is mentioned—possibly the patron of the manuscript.

ולא ביום יום ולא בבית יוסף ויתכוון בששת המעשה ושומר שיהא לו נעים ההולך בדרכי הש״ית ולא יתמיד להמותו וזה
וזהר כפי יכלתו ישלח להדיעו שכבת דיני ושאלה וקודם שישב לדוד ודע
וזה יעשה כל יום חייו הבלי יעיד יוסף כהנה לעשו טובה ויחיות שדי וישלים פרשיותיו
הצבור כל שמע שכם וזהר
ויחיד תרגם ואם יוכל יד
תהא יקרין מושכנו יום
ואף

הנה הסדר עד

זכרנו

לחיים מלך חפץ בחיים וכתבנו בספר החיים למענך אלהים חיים
מלך עוזר ומושיע ומגן ברוך אתה יי׳ מגן אברהם

אתה גבור לעולם יי׳ מחיה מתים אתה רב להושיע
מכלכל חיים בחסד מחיה מתים ברחמים רבים
סומך נופלים ורופא חולים ומתיר אסורים ומקיים
אמונתו לישני עפר מי כמוך בעל גבורות ומי דומה לך מלך ממית
ומחיה ומצמיח ישועה

מי כמוך אב הרחמים זוכר יצוריו לחיים
ברחמים ונאמן אתה להחיות מתים
בא״י מחיה המתים

ואף
הלכות שאין [illegible]
[illegible] ישרה
[illegible]
[illegible]
[illegible]
[illegible]
[illegible]
[illegible]
[illegible]
[illegible]
[illegible]
[illegible]
שלא יעשה סעודת שבת
וסמוך לערב יביא חטה
ושלחן וכסא ומנורה
ויכין הכל עסותו קערות
ויהיו זהיר בין לקידוש

היום ויעשו יספרנו בכל עניש וישתו סכנ׳ כי שדשו רז״ל והיה ביום הששי והכינו יותנו וזהו השחותם ויוצא
עבו ידיו ורגליו סרוק לעש ואחר שתקן כל ימים וכל זה שיעשה ימין לכבוד ולעונג שבת ויומיה וכן החיו על הקדש
וסרוק לחשיב ידישו בבגדיו וידליק נרות ועמד שהשרים מיום היוולן יקדש היום ויתפלל של שבת ויעזה ויתענג
ויסיר נולם כל יגעה וכל דאגה וכל וחשב סוו נעשת כל מלאכתו ויכבד שבת בכסות נקיי כי זה שיאל ויסעוד
ג׳ סעודו׳ משלחן ערוך ולא ידבר שום דבר והחפצין הצריכין לו ויתן מחפיב שהי וחשב מנות שיעמו חחם ולא יגע כ
שיהא יום ולא בזה שהי ומכבי תור כי זה בקדשי התורה דברי תורה ולא יפסיע פסיעה גסה ואם ולא ידבר כי זה וכל
טוחלות יעשה ולא ידבר ודוובו שיהיו וכל דברי הנכבד הלב מלו של דבר יקיים יום ענג ויום נפשה ולא יה

PLATE 39

Bible

fol. 137v *Frontispiece to Joshua*

A monumental arch frontispiece, framing the opening Hebrew text to Joshua, serves as an architectural gateway into this biblical book. Two classicizing, winged *putti* in the tympanum of the arch and under the coffered ceiling uphold the panel containing the initial gold Hebrew word of the book of Joshua *vayehi* ("*and it was. . . .*") Winged *putti,* festive garlands, and festoons surround the arch and its base. The artist has set the arch within a delicate, minutely painted landscape with buildings and mountains; he shows full mastery of vanishing point perspective. Wide, classicizing borders on either side display a rich array of *putti,* centaurs, animals, precious stone clusters, and candelabra motifs. Scattered between the strap-work ornamentation or written on scrolls above and below the central design are the Masoretic notes. The recessed archway and some of the decorative details are indeed comparable to the frontispiece with an archway painted by the famous Florentine artist Attavante (cf. his *Biblia dos Jeronymus,* now in the Lisbon National Library). However, the style of the figures does not point to Attavante. It may be, according to Mirella Levi D'Ancona, an early work of Jacopo del Giallo. The muscular *putti* in complicated poses and the modeling of heads suggest his style (cf. *Missal of Clement II* in London, Collection Jeudwine).

ויהי
אחרי מות משה עבד יהוה ויאמר יהוה אל יהושע
בן נון משרת משה לאמר׃ משה עבדי מת ועתה קום
עבר את הירדן הזה אתה וכל העם הזה אל הארץ
אשר אנכי נתן להם לבני ישראל׃ כל מקום אשר
תדרך כף רגלכם בו לכם נתתיו כאשר דברתי אל
משה׃ מהמדבר והלבנון הזה ועד הנהר הגדול נהר
פרת כל ארץ החתים ועד הים הגדול מבוא השמש
יהיה גבולכם׃ לא יתיצב איש לפניך כל ימי חייך
כאשר הייתי עם משה אהיה עמך לא ארפך ולא
אעזבך׃ חזק ואמץ כי אתה תנחיל את העם הזה את
הארץ אשר נשבעתי לאבותם לתת להם׃ רק חזק
ואמץ מאד לשמר לעשות ככל התורה אשר צוך
משה עבדי אל תסור ממנו ימין ושמאול למען
תשכיל בכל אשר תלך׃ לא ימוש ספר התורה
הזה מפיך והגית בו יומם ולילה למען תשמר
לעשות ככל הכתוב בו כי אז תצליח את דרכך

PLATE 40

Bible

fol. 374v *Frontispiece to Chronicles*

Written and partly decorated in Portugal, this manuscript reveals framed textual frontispieces to the books of the Bible. Apparently the scribe, who used the handsome square *Sephardi* script, left spaces for the artist to illuminate title pages to the books of the Hebrew Bible, but only two of eighteen selected folios were actually illuminated in Portugal (cf. fol. 9v to Genesis and this page, the Introduction to the Book of Chronicles). Seven sumptuously illuminated pages were obviously added in Italy (Plate 39). The two distinct artistic styles thus evident in this manuscript can probably be explained by the expulsion of unbaptized Jews from Portugal in 1496–1497. If this manuscript was begun in Lisbon before this date, the owner of the incomplete manuscript may have taken it with him to Italy and had it illuminated in his new home there.

Surrounding the framed text is a second frame which has a star pattern made of two intersecting squares. Set against a delicate filigree background is the centered Hebrew word *adam*—the opening word of the Book of Chronicles. The rest of the frame is filled with feathery scrolls on colored ground. In the third frame of the outer margin are gilded knobs and acanthus decorations, inhabited by such animals as birds, a stylized butterfly in the upper margin, a stylized rampant lion and a long-necked dragon with a human mask on its chest, both with scrolled leaves emanating from their mouths, in the lower margin. These latter animals flank a stylized spread peacock—a favorite motif in Portuguese Hebrew manuscripts, most made at Lisbon in the last quarter of the fifteenth century [cf. such dated Portuguese Hebrew manuscripts as London: British Library, Mss. Harley 5698–5699 (1472) and Mss. Or. 2626–2628 (1482)].

אדם

שֵׁת אֱנוֹשׁ׳ קֵינָן מַהֲלַלְאֵל יֶרֶד׳ חֲנוֹךְ מְתוּשֶׁלַח
לֶמֶךְ׳ נֹחַ שֵׁם חָם וָיֶפֶת בְּנֵי יֶפֶת גֹּמֶר וּמָגוֹג וּמָדַי וְיָוָן
וְתֻבָל וּמֶשֶׁךְ וְתִירָס׳ וּבְנֵי גֹמֶר אַשְׁכְּנַז וְרִיפַת
וְתֹגַרְמָה׳ וּבְנֵי יָוָן אֱלִישָׁה וְתַרְשִׁישָׁה כִּתִּים וְרוֹדָנִים
בְּנֵי חָם כּוּשׁ וּמִצְרַיִם פּוּט וּכְנָעַן וּבְנֵי כוּשׁ סְבָא
וַחֲוִילָה וְסַבְתָּא וְרַעְמָא וְסַבְתְּכָא וּבְנֵי רַעְמָה שְׁבָא
וּדְדָן וְכוּשׁ יָלַד אֶת נִמְרוֹד הוּא הֵחֵל לִהְיוֹת גִּבּוֹר
בָּאָרֶץ וּמִצְרַיִם יָלַד אֶת לוּדִים וְאֶת עֲנָמִים וְאֶת
לְהָבִים וְאֶת נַפְתֻּחִים וְאֶת פַּתְרֻסִים וְאֶת כַּסְלֻחִים
אֲשֶׁר יָצְאוּ מִשָּׁם פְּלִשְׁתִּים וְאֶת כַּפְתֹּרִים׳
וּכְנַעַן יָלַד אֶת צִידֹן בְּכֹרוֹ וְאֶת
חֵת׳ וְאֶת הַיְבוּסִי וְאֶת הָאֱמֹרִי וְאֶת הַגִּרְגָּשִׁי׳ וְאֶת
הַחִוִּי וְאֶת הָעַרְקִי וְאֶת הַסִּינִי׳ וְאֶת הָאַרְוָדִי׳ וְאֶת
הַצְּמָרִי וְאֶת הַחֲמָתִי׳ בְּנֵי שֵׁם עֵילָם וְאַשּׁוּר׳ ע׳
וְאַרְפַּכְשַׁד וְלוּד וְאֲרָם וְעוּץ וְחוּל וְגֶתֶר וָמֶשֶׁךְ׳ וצ׳

40